GEORGIA
COVERED
BRIDGES

GEORGIA
COVERED
BRIDGES

LISA M. RUSSELL

THE
History
PRESS

Published by The History Press
Charleston, SC
www.historypress.com

Cover art by Charlotte McDonnell from Roswell, Georgia.

First published 2023

Manufactured in the United States

ISBN 9781467153843

Library of Congress Control Number: 2023937163

Notice: The information in this book is true and complete to the best of our knowledge. It is offered without guarantee on the part of the author or The History Press. The author and The History Press disclaim all liability in connection with the use of this book.

For Wheeler David Russell
Be a mighty man of God and do great things.

I have found in David the son of Jesse a man after my heart,
who will do all my will.
—Acts 13:22, ESV

CONTENTS

PREFACE

S eriously—covered bridges? Not a deep subject. It will not take a lot of research, and it will be a quick project. Right.

My husband first suggested I write about bridges in North Georgia. He has a nostalgic view of those iron and concrete structures. I wanted to finish my "Lost" series and write about the lost mills in Fulton County since I had so much left over from my *Lost Mills of North Georgia* book. The History Press allowed me to author a fourth book about lost things. They wanted me to write about the covered bridges in Georgia. I must admit that it underwhelmed me, but I went forth.

Despite my reluctance, I began researching these structures because everyone else wanted to know more. So, I began my research and visits. The more work I did, the more invested I became; I was excited to see this through. Going to a covered bridge is essential to understanding a time gone by. I am always going to the places I am trying to write about, and this was no different. For the bridges I could not travel to because of my schedule and responsibilities at home, I spent a great deal of time watching other people experience them with drones and video.

I discovered that while there is a lot of information online about our bridges, you need to be careful because fake news abounds. We have lost the facts among clickbait and beautiful images. I found it confusing to untangle the conflicting numbers and figure out what was a historic bridge and what was a reproduction. It took some time for me to get the bridges straight in my head, much like when I have a classroom of college students and never remember their names.

On this journey, I got to visit my beloved theme of lost things. I used my research to uncover what happened to these lost bridges. I used My Maps to create a map that allowed me to visualize the enormity of what we lost and to click between what we lost and what survived. You can find that map and interact with it. I created a QR code along with a simplified map in the back of the book in the chapter called "Road Trip and the Purpose of Place."

This trip differed from earlier journeys in writing about Georgia's history. Yeah, I thought it was going to be easier. There were fewer researched sources to find. But I had to look in different places and talk to more people. I even had to break down and finally subscribe to Newspapers.com to find stories about the bridges in the communities where they exist. I hope you enjoy reading about these magical places and getting to know them. See how valuable they are, and if you have a chance, help preserve them for your children and grandchildren.

ACKNOWLEDGMENTS

D eadlines. I am notoriously late and love the sound of that date passing me by. My husband thinks I love the thrill of rushing toward the finish line. Maybe. It is exhausting trying to write about true things. The best part of writing is having written, and the second best is the hunt. I love researching and finding hidden things in old newspapers, archives and conversations with actual experts. So, I must thank those who helped me get the facts straight. Some I have never met except through their research and expertise. Thomas French and Edward French wrote the 1984 book *Covered Bridges of Georgia*, which is the beginning of my search outside the internet. This treasure, along with anything else written by the Frenches, guaranteed accuracy. Their work allowed me to see the covered bridges of Georgia from an architect's perspective.

Be careful online when researching anything to make sure your sources are credible. I sound like the English professor I am, but Googling does not find some of the best sources. There are some exceptions. I watched many YouTube videos by fellow travelers that took me to bridges I could not visit and old videos of bridges being moved and their stories told. So many people are passionate about our covered bridges, and I am grateful they pulled out a drone or a GoPro to chronicle their travel stories.

One online resource was not only credible but also essential to my search for those lost bridges. The National Society for the Preservation of Covered Bridges does an amazing job of providing accurate data and pointing to credible sources. To learn more about covered bridges across the country, go to www.coveredbridgesociety.org/aboutus.html.

Other local experts were invaluable, beginning with retired Georgia Department of Transportation engineer Paul Liles. He pointed me in all the right directions at the beginning of this journey. Here are just a few who helped with the production of this book:

Lori Hamby, park manager at Watson Mill Bridge State Park, encouraged me on that long rainy day when I visited the bridge. Great gift shop!

Philip Ivester, Patricia Burns, Robert Roche and especially Dave Mahloy at the Concord Bridge and Ruff's Mill Group.

It always begins at home when I start a project to see if Trey Gaines, director of the Bartow History Museum, has anything to add to my research.

I dislike going to these hidden places alone. Thank you, Lisa Miller, for going with me to explore the Historic Concord Bridge and Ruff's Mill.

Jimmy and Martha McConnell, thank you for meeting me at Poole's Mill. They went above and beyond as co-presidents of the Historical Society of Cumming/Forsyth County.

Michael Prochazka, editor of the *Oconee Enterprise*, for answering my questions about Elder's Mill and the "Bridge Troll."

Again and again, the Atlanta History Center at Kenan Research has helped me find those rare things.

Lewis O. Powell IV as research archivist for clearing up some things about the bridge Horace King built in Troup County.

Thank you, Katie O. Gobbi, community development director for the City of Euharlee, who answered my last-minute fact checks so fast.

Thank you to Vickie and David McEntire for their beautiful covered bridge images and another great headshot I can use over and over.

And to my sons, John and Samuel, thank you for jump-starting this journey on a long trip to George L. Smith State Park to see my first covered bridge for this book.

To my friend Ella, who always prays even when she has so much going on in her life.

To my husband for putting up with all the time I have to spend writing and revising and not cooking—wait, I do not like to cook even when I am not writing!

I get to welcome another daughter into my family this year and along with her comes her wonderful family. Elisabeth's mother is a gifted artist. Charlotte McDonnell painted the cover of this book of Euharlee Covered Bridge. What a humbling gift to have someone share their talent in this way. Thank you, Charlotte. I look forward to a future project for our grandkids.

And finally, and always, my thanks to our creative God, who has allowed me to write and given me the strength to carry on. He has been my "agent" at every opportunity and has given me purpose in all of this. I just heard a new song by my favorite singer/songwriter, Amy Grant. I thought about writing all this history and how these lines apply to this purpose-driven life:

> *We're all sons and daughters, just ripples on the water*
> *Tryna make it matter until our time to leave*
> *One day, they'll carve your name in stone*
> *And send your soul on home*
> *'Til then it's prayin' for rain and pullin' up the weeds*
> *Plantin' trees we'll never see*
> —*Amy Grant, "Trees We'll Never See"*

INTRODUCTION

Covered bridges are misunderstood, and the internet does not help. Trying to find the truth has been surprisingly difficult for a topic I thought would be straightforward. The more I learned about these bridges, the more I ran into conflicting information. All the superlatives describing the bridges had to be weighed and confirmed. For example, is Red Oak Covered Bridge really the oldest bridge, and was it built by the famous bridge builder Horace King? Is Watson Mill really the longest bridge in Georgia and the United States? How many historic bridges exist in our state? The number feels fluid.

One big question has some silly answers: why are these bridges covered? Here are some of the false answers for covering bridges:

- They covered the bridges so the cows could cross without fear.
- The covered bridges allowed for all that heavy Georgia snow to fall off easily.
- They built covered bridges for romance. A skillful horseman could train his horse to cross the bridge slowly so he could steal a kiss while in the semi-dark tunnel.

So, what is the reason for covering bridges? The answer is simple—it is good business. The covering saves the bridge from decaying from the inside out. The engineering allowed many of the century-old bridges to remain standing today. From the early 1800s to the early 1900s, these bridges provided safe transportation for goods to get to market and people to move about in early Georgia. Fording a creek or ferrying across the rivers was dangerous and costly for progress.

We will document their progress in the following chapters and explain who constructed these timber tunnels and how they were constructed. We will get to know the 16 remaining historical bridges still standing across Georgia. This number has changed from decade to decade. At one time, Georgia had over 250 covered bridges. By 1955, that number had shrunk to 75. In the 1970s, only 25 remained. Thanks to preservationists and Georgia's Department of Transportation, 16 historic bridges endured. Today, the number changes from person to person. People report the covered bridge number from 13 to 17, but the true number is sweet 16. We will look at a few of the lost bridges of Georgia and figure out where some of them went. In addition, we will take a brief look at the other bridges that are not historical but sometimes get added to the list of authentic covered bridges.

Here in this book is an introduction to bridge builders. These nineteenth-century bridge engineers trademarked designs that still stand today. One builder was an enslaved apprentice who out-built his master. Horace King honored his master and their friendship by placing a monument next to his grave. This act earned King a place in *Ripley's Believe It or Not*.

But there must be more to this book than discussing data and bridge design. I want this book to be more than a travel guide. I want it to differ from anything else out there. The thing I want for you out of this book is to get to know these places. I want you to know the personality of each bridge that survived. Each is unique with local history; you cannot take these bridges out of their context. Moving some of these structures only added to their character. When I started researching this book, I could not match the pictures to the names. But then I got to know each survivor. I visited them and watched videos about them, and now I know them with all their backstories. And I mourn the lost bridges of Georgia.

There is poetry in bridges; they are a metaphor. In the old language, a metaphor was a bridge from one meaning to another. Poet Philip Larkin writes, "Always it is by bridges that we live."[1] Poetry and bridges can transition from something known to something mysterious. Think of all the clichés about bridges that are spiritual, such as "Like a Bridge over Troubled Water." Or when we are trying to transition to something new and let things go: "It's water under the bridge." Bridges are magical, exciting, different and scary.

One thing I have consistently heard from people inquiring about my current writing project is, "Oh, covered bridges are so romantic." I never understood that unless they really loved Clint Eastwood and Meryl Streep in *The Bridges of Madison County*. Maybe it is just the spiritual metaphor that taps into our souls. We want our lives to have meaning, and the phrase "a bridge to nowhere" is disconcerting. We want our lives to go somewhere—anywhere.

Recently, I heard a new perspective on bridges from a modern bridge designer. Ian Firth said this in a TED Talk: "Bridges are not just about a safe way across a river or an obstacle. They shout about connectivity, and community…they reveal something about creativity, our ingenuity. They even hint at our identity."[2]

In his poem "The Bridge," Shel Silverstein invites us to walk on: "So come and walk awhile with me and share the twisting trails and wondrous worlds I've known. But this bridge will only take you halfway there—the last few steps you'll have to take alone." Enjoy your journey as you discover the covered bridges of Georgia. Walk on.

PART I

THE BUILDERS
AND THE BUILDS

Chapter 1

PATENT HOLDERS

I n early Georgia, settlers had to ford streams and creeks on horses with wagons. Larger rivers required ferries. When the waters rose, so did the danger. Before 1800, with little more than Native American pig trails, transportation was difficult and commerce was near impossible. Georgians needed to look to northern engineers for answers. They had already discovered that stone structures were expensive and simple wood crossings did not last.

Andrea Palladio, an Italian architect of the post-Renaissance, drew the first published plans for "wooden bridge trusses" in the 1500s. Palladio's design influenced an eccentric American bridge builder, Timothy Palmer. Palmer, a self-taught Massachusetts bridge builder, had a new idea. He had been building uncovered bridges using trussed arch designs that made the structures stable. He added a covering to extend their lifespan and protect the investment. Soon, other builders were using roofs and siding even on small bridges.[3]

History credits Palmer as the builder of America's first covered bridge. The Permanent Bridge, which he constructed over the Schuylkill River in Philadelphia, Pennsylvania, opened to traffic on January 1, 1805. The aptly named Permanent Bridge had three arch-supported trusses; two were 150 feet long, and the other was 195 feet long. Because of the $300,000 price tag, the bridge was covered to protect the city's investment. The builder expected it to last about forty to fifty years. Expanded to accommodate a railroad in 1850, it remained in service until fire destroyed it on November 20, 1875. Palmer discovered that covering the bridge could extend its life seven to eight times. This explains why any of the historic Georgia bridges are still standing today.[4]

Theodore Burr of Terring Ford, Connecticut, patented his Burr truss in 1804. He built dozens of bridges in the Northeast. He overextended himself by accepting a contract for five Burr arch truss bridges over the Susquehanna River in Pennsylvania. This caused Burr to lose everything and die early in 1822.[5]

Ithiel Town (1784–1844) was the most famous and prolific truss designer. Most of the surviving Georgia bridges were built with Town lattice trusses. Town was born in Thompson, Connecticut, and built with the Burr truss until he invented his own. He designed and patented the lattice truss in 1820. It was a simple design that any building crew could use to complete contracts on time and within budget.

Town's trusses acted as load-bearing beams to reduce stress on the piers and abutments. Town's design allowed for a cost-effective way to put up a bridge quickly in a growing area with little labor and cheap materials. Wood was plentiful, and the truss system would allow the bridges with covers or roofs to outlast the elements. The covered bridge design was so enduring that only fires, floods and later vandalism could bring them down. According to author French, Town changed his design by placing two treenails at every

Red Oak Creek Covered Bridge, spanning (Big) Red Oak Creek and Huel Brown Road (Covered Bridge Road), Woodbury, Meriwether County. The insides, north portal. Note the board-and-batten siding. *LOC. HAER GA-138-4.*

Watson Mill Covered Bridge. Internal portal, eastern end. Watson Mill Bridge State Park, Comer, Madison/Oglethorpe County. *LOC. HAER GA-140-14.*

junction of the diagonals and the stringer. The Cheraw Bridge showed this modification by 1824.[6]

Ithiel Town had a neighbor who shared his passion for innovation and the South. Eli Whitney, the co-inventor of the cotton gin, came up with a way to profit further from the gin.[7] He tried to franchise his design. He charged builders one dollar per foot for using his design. For builders who did not pay, he charged them two dollars per foot. Wonder how he collected that fee? In a strange coincidence, Town sent Whitney a model of his lattice-designed bridge. Maybe that is how Town got the idea to franchise his covered bridge design. Town tried to maximize his profit like Whitney did the cotton gin.[8]

Colonel Stephen Harriman Long's truss design (1784) resembled a series of giant boxed *X*s. This design was the first wooden truss in the United States to require mathematical calculations.

William Howe (1803–1852) patented his truss in 1840. The Howe truss was so similar to the Long truss that Howe was accused of infringement. Howe had replaced the upright wooden post in Long's design with adjustable iron rods. Introducing iron rods may have been the beginning of the end for the wooden tunnels.[9]

Chapter 2

EARLY PRACTITIONERS

S lave owner Edward King died, and John Godwin either inherited
Horace King and his family or outright purchased them. Either way,
Godwin treated Horace with respect, and they worked together to
build bridges and an empire. Horace King was building a bridge to his
freedom.

John Godwin (1798–1859) was an early bridge builder in Georgia from the
Cheraw District of South Carolina. He was from a prominent landholding
family who owned a small resort town west of the Pee Dee River called
Sneedsboro.

Horace King was born enslaved in 1807. His father, Edmund, was a
light-skinned enslaved man. Horace's mother was part Catawba Indian.
Somewhere in his childhood, he learned how to read and write. He had an
excellent mind for engineering.

Later in life, King told his story in his own words. In 1878, he said, "I
was born in South Carolina a Slave, the property of Edward King. He died,
and his heirs sold me to Jennings Dunlop of Cheraw. He sold me to John
Godwin."

John Godwin was a local builder in the growing Cheraw community. He
could have made enough money building homes to purchase Horace King
and his family. This transaction occurred between 1828 and 1832. The
1830 census showed Godwin owned seven slaves. While building a family
home in Cheraw, John Godwin and his worker Horace King had to cross
the muddy Pee Dee River. The bridge had washed away in 1826, so Godwin

and King were contracted to rebuild the bridge in 1828 to complete home construction. Either King had construction skills or Godwin apprentice him, but somewhere along the way, the pair learned Ithiel Town's method of bridge building.[10] They might have watched as Town supervised its building.

The original 1824 bridge served as a model for the rebuilt bridge. The *Cheraw Intelligencer and Southern Register* wrote an over-the-top description of the new bridge on June 18, 1824: "This grand and extensive work across the Pee Dee River opposite this place is now completed…constructed on the self-supporting principle invented by Mr. Ithiel Town.…In point of elegance and extent, it by far surpasses any in this State, and is believed to be little inferior to any in the Union."[11]

Lupold and French, in their book *Bridging Deep South Rivers*, describe this early process. The bridge over Pee Dee rose from the clay bottom once cofferdams diverted the waters. Then enslaved workers "hewed beams as other hands bored holes in the multitude of sawn pine or cypress boards that became the timber tunnel held together by hardwood treenails." Treenails are wooden nails that hold the bridge together. Machine-made nails did not exist in the 1820s, so workers pegged the framing together with treenails.

Town's trusses acted as load-bearing beams to reduce stress on the piers and abutments. His design allowed for a cost-effective way to put up a bridge quickly in a growing area with little labor and inexpensive materials. Wood was plentiful, and using the truss system would allow the bridges with covers or roofs to outlast the elements.

Thomas French described Ithiel Town's patented trusses as "crossed braces or diagonals sandwiched between horizontal stringers or chords." He also explained, "Town quickly changed his design by placing two treenails at every junction of the diagonals and the stringer; this modification appeared in the Cheraw bridge by 1824."[12]

The South was littered with small rivers that used ferries for commerce. Communities grew up along these waterways and would petition state legislatures for bridge construction. The need for bridges grew as cotton needed to be brought to market. Investors rather than municipalities financed mostly bridges.

The Cheraw Bridge Company, formed by Godwin, built unique but utilitarian bridges across small waterways. Wagons loaded with cotton and produce crossed these bridges and grew the early southern American economy.[13]

Godwin, like many men in the 1800s, moved west, which meant Columbus, Georgia. In January 1832, the New Columbus Council advertised for a builder for a bridge over the Chattahoochee to replace a ferry, and Godwin bid on it.[14] In 1830, Columbus was a rugged frontier with random roads and buildings. The residents, however, wanted to become a major cotton-trading town because it was on the Chattahoochee River, with Alabama just a ferry ride away. In 1831, interested in improving trade, the Georgia legislature loaned Columbus $16,000 to build a bridge across the Chattahoochee. The town began accepting sealed bids from bridge builders. Godwin found out the amount the legislature loaned Columbus and bid under but did not make a model like other builders. He was counting on the reputation of the Town lattice design. The city accepted John Godwin's bid.

Godwin established himself with King in Alabama in Indian territory, later named Girard. They were in a pioneering town and got many contracts for small bridges, houses, factories and warehouses. They built five major bridges across the Chattahoochee River in ten years. King built his reputation by constructing the first Columbus bridge in 1832, City Bridge. His reputation for craftsmanship and completing the job grew.

Godwin would leave King to work on other projects and invest in a sure thing: a railroad in this pioneering place. King was hired to complete projects that other builders abandoned. He soon was building bridges all over Georgia. He built five bridges in Columbus alone. He and Godwin guaranteed their work for five years, so if flood or fire came, they rebuilt.

In 1839, the builders won a contract to build a bridge across the Chattahoochee near West Point, Georgia. This project would change Horace King's life. While most Creek Indians had moved west, a few had remained, and many of those were adopted into non-Indian families. King married Frances Thomas, a free African American woman with Creek and white blood. Thomas was fourteen. Most important was that Frances was a free woman. King knew any children they had would be born free. They had five children who survived into adulthood. His four sons learned his trade. This family business included his only daughter.

Horace King's early story and his path to freedom story are sketchy. In 1876, King said he had bought his freedom in 1848. Legislators in Alabama and Georgia passed laws in 1846 allowing this, so his memory might have been unclear on this.

Family lore confuses the story even more when told in some biographies that Godwin sent King to Oberlin College in Ohio. There is no supporting evidence of this, according to the bridge biographer Thomas French. Despite this fallacy, Godwin apprenticed King, who became a better entrepreneur than his former master. King ultimately succeeded beyond Godwin.

Horace King worked hard for John Godwin, and in his own words in 1878, "I learned the trade of bridge building. Worked at leisure time, made money, and bought my freedom in 1848 and have since been engaged in bridge building."[15]

People are still asking how Godwin freed King. Some stories say Godwin gave him his freedom, while others say he met a building deadline and earned it. But Horace said he paid the purchase price.

According to southern laws, freed slaves could be responsible for their former masters' debts at the time of their freedom. Godwin had substantial debt. While King was keeping his bridge business growing, Godwin was making poor investments in a railroad line. His finances were underwater. Godwin's family, however, made sure that Horace King was not responsible for that debt. They took legal action to make sure King was clear. The Russell County Courthouse declared Horace King emancipated and freed from all claims. Horace would never forget it.

Whatever the truth, King earned a place in *Ripley's Believe It or Not* for paying $300 ($10,813.37 today) for a monument for John Godwin's grave.[16] King was grateful not only for Godwin's apprenticeship but also for his not selling Horace when he needed cash.

King took care of the Godwin family and even allowed John's daughter to have his large house while he lived in her small house. He lived in gratitude for all John Godwin did for him. He expressed it on a granite stone in a Godwin gravesite King set aside. The memorial read:

> *John Godwin*
> *Born Oct. 17, 1798. Died on Feb. 26, 1859.*
> *This stone was placed here by Horace King,*
> *in lasting remembrance of the love and gratitude*
> *he felt for his lost friend and former master.*

The stone still stands in Phenix City, Alabama, two miles from their first bridge project, City Bridge (later called Dillingham), in the Godwin Cemetery. This was an unusual friendship. John Godwin gave Horace King and his family a chance to thrive by giving him a trade. He gave him a life in an unlikely place and at an unusual time.

Chapter 3

THE KING BUILDING COMPANY

Horace King and his sons formed their own construction company, King & Co. Later, the brothers incorporated King Brothers Co. and built bridges all over Georgia. Horace worked on an important project when he built a floating staircase in the Alabama statehouse in 1850. His reputation kept him busy, and his work on the stairs led to other opportunities. The staircase was deconstructed one hundred years later in the 1950s, and workers exposed King's unique building method, explaining why all his projects lasted longer than most wood constructions. King could not have known that within a few years of this statehouse construction, he would be elected to serve in that same statehouse. After the Civil War, King reluctantly served as a representative in the "Black and Tan" era of Reconstruction politics. He made friends with powerful politicians who could help him get building jobs. These powerful men also kept Horace King and his sons out of harm's way during and after the war.

The Civil War was a dilemma for Horace. He did not want slavery to continue, but he wanted the South to survive. King's friendship with Alabama politician Robert Jemison kept him and his sons working in the Naval Iron Works. The Columbus location was a safe and neutral place to wait for the war's end. After the war, King was busy rebuilding all the burned bridges and buildings. His political friend Jemison encouraged King to run for state office. During Reconstruction, Black men were encouraged to do so. King was not an enthusiastic politician and did not campaign, but he won two terms. Horace King accomplished significant things while in office.

The Horace King family of builders and contractors. *Courtesy of Schomburg Center for Research in Black Culture, Jean Blackwell Hutson Research and Reference Division, the New York Public Library.*

For the rest of his life, even after he moved to LaGrange, Georgia, he served the community—especially freedmen.[17]

Frances King died in 1864, and King married Sarah Jane McManus in 1869. He moved his business to LaGrange in 1872. It is not clear why they moved, but a local paper recognized his son Washington W. "W.W." King's work, though in condescending and racial tones. The May 13, 1883 *Atlanta-Constitution* article announced:

> *King & Co. have put their various works in motion and received their first building contract from the city—a neat pavilion for the cemetery. King is a colored man, a son of the famous Horace King, and inherits his sire's*

remarkable gifts in the mechanism. He has a white man's principles and is
highly respected.[18]

Horace died in 1885, and for a long time, the location of his gravesite was a mystery. His grave was misplaced for years, and when it was found, his date of death was incorrect. He was buried next to his son Marshall, who died before him. They discovered the graves and placed a new memorial. Horace King was further honored in 2021. Troup County loaded up the Callaway Garden Covered Bridge and moved it back home to his grave (read about this in the Wehadkee Covered Bridge chapter). The bridge was rebuilt in 2023, and a park and memorials honoring Horace King are being created.

His son Washington W. King moved his business, Bridge Co., to Atlanta and built various structures in Georgia. He was recently honored with the naming of a bridge at Stone Mountain. The bridge that was moved in the 1960s from Athens to Stone Mountain State Park was W.W. King's work (read about this in the Washington W. King Covered Bridge chapter). People noticed the irony when the bridge was renamed Washington W. King in 2021. The King Bridge sits in the shadow of the Stone Mountain carving remembering the Civil War. We are long past this point in history, or we should be. However, in a 1988 Phenix City Alabama Council session, Arthur Sumbry suggested they name the North Bypass Bridge after Horace King. Crickets. Thomas French, the King biographer, rightly said, "Had Horace King been a white man, everybody would have known who he was."[19]

Chapter 4

DIRT DAUBERS AND DABBLERS

A spring flash flood came to Settendown Creek under Poole's Mill Covered Bridge, and B.L. Fowler hired John Wofford to repair the flooded bridge. He sawed the lumber out of heart poplar and prepared to rebuild using the Town's lattice design. But Wofford made a mistake in boring the holes. He was mad at his mistake and got a gallon of corn whiskey and took off. Fowler had to hire Bud Gentry to finish the job.

Georgia employed some successful bridge builders and some who did subpar work. The longevity of their builds is evidence. But those who built with quality plans have standing legacies. You will read about them as I have recorded their names in the bridge chapters and even in the lost bridge chapter. Some were students of the Kings. J.M. Hunt built Howard's and Cromer's Bridges, and Washington King taught him. Hunt's bridges have stood the test of time.

Mill owners or other private businesses contracted the most bridges. Local community officials hired some, and some were in business for themselves, like the ferry operators. The name they were given is "dirt daubers." According to Thomas French, dirt daubers are industrious builders. These bridge builders were named for the insect. They were entrepreneurs who built bridges and charged tolls.[20]

French said of these bridge builders:

> *They came from all walks of life; doctors, lawyers, judges, and one was a slave. In the construction of their bridges, these men had very limited*

A mistake was made by the contractor at Poole's Mill Covered Bridge. He cut holes in the wrong place, and then he got drunk, got mad and quit the job. *Author's photo.*

equipment, diesel-powered backhoes, cranes, and bulldozers were unheard of. The bridge builder of the 1800s could not move mountains or relocate streams to accommodate their needs; the lay of the land dictated the bridge location. When it came down to the actual construction, the tools were few and crude, but native skills and pioneering virtue of these early bridge builders have left us a legacy in wood.[21]

Chapter 5

HOW TO BUILD A BRIDGE

O ne of my favorite lessons to teach my freshman English students is when we are learning about expository writing. To teach process writing, I show them gross food videos like how companies produce hot dogs or what is really in Chicken McNuggets. We gain foundations in the most mundane when we learn how to make something. Understanding these relics requires us to learn how an almost two-hundred-year-old bridge was built by using only the trees surrounding the building site.

I do not intend this book as a building manual. An expert can find the fine details of bridge construction and design elsewhere. This explains the parts of the bridge that help tell the story. For the narrative to make sense, you need a few details to honor these little tunnels of timber and pieces of history.

So here are the basics, with wording help from the National Society for the Preservation of Covered Bridges (NSPCB).[22] For definitions and more details, see the chapter "Bridge Words: Glossary." A covered bridge is a timber truss bridge that has a roof, a deck and siding. Most covered bridges create a nearly complete enclosure. Some call them "timber tunnels." The covering on the bridge is designed to protect the bridge and extend its lifespan. According to NSPCB, "Uncovered wooden bridges usually only last about twenty years before needing to be repaired or replaced, while covered wooden bridges can last as long as a century before any work needs to be done on them."[23]

An interesting thought is that these old bridges are still used. The nature of this type of wood construction makes them better with age. The tension,

Elder Mill Covered Bridge markings for Town's lattice truss building design. *Author's collection.*

Town lattice truss in Red Oak Covered Bridge. *LOC.*

Red Oak Covered Bridge view of decking from the underside with the concrete pier, Meriwether County. *LOC. HAER GA-138-11, HAER GA-138-8.*

compression and flex used in covered bridges stay supple and safe. Maybe, like aging joints, they need to be used.

You may wonder why some of the longer bridges have windows built into the sides. A long bridge can be dark, but the windows help with lighting. While they also limit privacy for romantics, they most likely helped provide ventilation for the wood timbers. With covered bridges, it is all about preserving the structure.

Horace King, formerly an enslaved artisan, had a specific process for bridge building. In the Euharlee bridge, you can still see the marking his son Washington left to piece together his puzzle-like construction. Horace and his sons perfected prefabricating first on the bank and then assembling.

King had all the pieces laid out and ready before he would lay the first piece of wood on the piers. This made it easier when a deal went south. Municipalities and private businesses contracted bridges. The Kings started one project in Milledgeville, Georgia, and the town could not decide about some aspects of the build. So Horace loaded a train with his prefabricated bridge walls and went to Albany to put up another bridge using those materials. He was a serious builder, and he did not suffer fools.

WHAT DID GDOT DO?

Bridge-loving Georgians owe a debt of gratitude to the preservationists at the Georgia Department of Transportation (GDOT). Under the leadership of its chief engineer, Paul Liles Jr., this organization has restored the covered bridges deemed historic. Most of the remaining historic covered bridges would have been lost if not for this retired state bridge engineer. Liles was the second-longest-serving bridge engineer in the state, as he served at GDOT for twenty-two years. This Georgia Tech civic engineer had many projects, but saving the historic bridges is his lasting legacy.

The Covered Bridge Project began in 1990 and lasted for ten years. Enhanced monies were used to put the bridges back to their original states, with some improvements. The old tin was replaced with cedar-shingled roofs. Lights were added for safety, and one bridge was given a sprinkler system.

Euharlee Covered Bridge boasts its own sprinkler system. Arson was popular, as you can see from the lost bridges listed, but lightning also played a part. Now there is less danger in fires because debris has been kept away from the bridges, as it is kindling for a fire.

Liles says most covered bridges in Georgia are owned by the counties where they exist because there is no real traffic on these bridges. Authentic covered bridges are not wide enough or structurally engineered to handle today's traffic. Very few allow traffic, and most had to be rebuilt to support traffic. Workers enhanced Cobb's almost urban Concord Covered Bridge with some steel, but it is still mostly a wood structure.

The bridge engineer exposes the myths of covered bridges. He also answers the question, "Why did they build a covered bridge during the 1800s?" Some think bridges were covered because the farmer did not want to get wet. Maybe the cows and horses were afraid of the rushing water below. Here is the truth: covered bridges were wood-sided trusses holding up the bridge. The principal support of the truss is wooden. The covered bridge was strong with wood construction, but the wood needed to be protected from rot and other damage to the structure of the bridge. Liles says, "It is easy to replace rotten boards on the sides or replace the roof." Termites and fire have been an issue for Georgia bridges. Lula Covered Bridge near Helen had termites when GDOT intervened. With a covering, like in a house, the interior remains strong and can last years longer than in an open bridge.

Original bridge builders did not foresee modern vehicles that are wider and heavier. Most need steel supports to allow modern traffic. Concord Bridge and Watson Mill State Park still allow traffic, but the state parks have an advantage over the county bridges. Bridges in state parks are under state control, and the state controls the traffic and closes it down at night. There is no such oversight for bridges like Concord. Stand near the bridge during rush hour when impatient drivers wait their turn. Only one bridge, the isolated Elder's Mill, still carries traffic without the support of steel beams.

According to Liles, before departments of transportation or highway departments, counties hired bridge builders, and the county maintained the bridges. Roads were difficult to navigate before 1916. Roads were built to towns and cities, but connecting them within the state was a mess. With the better roads movement in 1916, there was a debate—how should they pay for improved roads, and who would maintain them?

There was no income tax, and the Constitution only says there must be post roads; there is nothing about paying for roads. The government finally approved a gas tax and gave the monies to states. This was the beginning of early departments of transportation that would take care of the roads and bridges. The federal money could not go to a county. In Georgia, GDOT was born, and it took care of the aging bridges by restoring them to their earlier glory and then returning them to the counties.[24]

Elder's Mill Covered Bridge over Rose Creek in Oconee County. *Author photo, February 2023.*

Gerald M. Ross, GDOT chief engineer from 2007 to 2012 and interim commissioner in 2009, was part of the project to restore covered bridges. He said it was more of a historical project than a transportation project. Ten of the sixteen remaining bridges were restored by GDOT. Ross said they required the contractors on the project to use the same techniques that the original builders used over one hundred years ago. He said, "I couldn't imagine." As a college-trained bridge designer, he did not understand how these builders did it with tiny hammers and no crane while working across a river like the Chattahoochee.[25]

The Intermodal Surface Transportation Efficiency Act of 1991 (ISTEA) was a transportation enhancement program established to "enrich the traveling experience through enhancements to the transportation system." As part of this program, the Federal Highway Administration (FHWA) provided 80 percent matching funds for eligible projects. Georgia let $1,592,521 worth of work repairing the bridges (listed below), and all repairs were complete by September 1999. The program was so successful that the FHWA allocated an additional $10 million nationwide for rehabilitation in other states.

THE ORIGINAL PLANS FOR EACH BRIDGE

Coheelee Creek Bridge

Replace missing or damaged roof beams with 5x9 pine. Tie-down beams with steel rods to match the original rods (using the original rods where feasible). Replace the existing metal roof with a wood shingle roof. Replace at the end after the southeast corner of the bridge. Consolidate termite-damaged areas with epoxy as directed by the engineer. Replace missing nuts at trusses. Replace the bent rod to match the existing. Reinstall diagonal knee braces between posts and corresponding roof beams with 4x6 No. 2 pine. Replace missing or damaged weatherboarding battens to match existing sizes. Replace weatherboarding and battens at the south end of the bridge. Trim the board and the battens at the bottom to a uniform length. Clean earth from beams. Reinforce beams. Replace damaged purlins with 6x10 pine. Replace the existing metal roof with wood. Replace 5 feet of the treads on the east side of both ends of the bridge. A contract was awarded for this project for $128,007.

Concord Covered Bridge

Repair of damaged framing and weatherboarding at the east gable. Application of wood preservative to the exterior of the bridge. Install a set of new treads at the floor of the bridge. Cut back paving and remove earth from the ends of the bridge. Install a trench drain to separate the bridge structure from the earth and pavement. Repair a crack in the center stone pier. Install new height restrictors at the end of the bridge. Provisions also shall be made for the installation of new electrical service and lighting at the ends and interior of the bridge. The contract for $151,188 was let in September 1998.

Cromer's Mill Bridge

Replace the existing metal roof. Replace missing or broken cross-bracing members at ceiling beams. Secure all connections of cross-members to beams. Replace missing and broken weatherboarding to match the existing. Apply wood preservative to the exterior of the bridge to protect weatherboarding.

Shore up the east truss and the replacement of the broken chord members at the pole support. Replace deteriorated chord members at the north end of the bridge. Replace six broken lattice members. Repair the truss at the north end where the truss has been shortened. Replace chin braces. Reinforce the connections of all chin braces to the top chord; Attach all chin braces at the bottom. Replace damaged or deteriorated floor decking and treads. Install flat board at the edge of the floor to cover the gap between the flooring and chord of truss. Replace six floor joists. Construct a new concrete pier at the north end of the bridge. Provision of a new sole plate and heel plate to support trusses. Repair the existing pier at the south end of the bridge. Form and pour a concrete cap on top of the pier. Excavate the earthen approach on the north end of the bridge. Construct a new abutment and wooden approach at the north end. Remove the existing approach at the south end of the bridge and excavate earth behind the existing pier. Construct a new abutment and wooden approach at the south end. Place a concrete bollard at each end of the bridge. The contract for this project was let in September 1998 for $147,815.

Elder's Mill Covered Bridge

Replace broken ceiling beams to match the originals. Replace broken cross-bracing members at ceiling beams and secure all connections of cross-bracing members to beams. Apply wood preservative to the exterior of the bridge to protect weatherboarding. Replace four lattice members and consolidate termite-damaged areas with epoxy. Replace four chin braces and reinforce the connections of all chin braces to the top chord and their attachment to the bottom. Add horizontal guard rails to each end of the bridge to prevent oversized vehicles from reaching the bridge. Replace damaged floor decking and treads. Replace damaged floor beams to match the originals. Provide for steel hangars at all beams. Replace broken cross-bracing members at floor beams. Secure all connections of cross-breaking members to beams. Remove accumulated dirt between sole plates and atop piers. Remove earth from around all wood structure at approaches. Repair all damaged wood members. Construct a trench drain system along the end of the approach to separate the wood structure from the earth. Treat the abutment areas for termites. Provisions also shall be made for the installation of electrical service and bridge lighting. The contract for this project was let in April 1997 for $162,030.

Euharlee Creek Bridge

Inspect the metal roof to identify panels that need replacement. Apply an asphaltic coating to prolong the roof's life. Replace broken or damaged ceiling beams to match originals. Replace missing or broken cross-bracing members at the ceiling beams. Secure all connections of cross-bracing members to the beams. Replace missing or broken weatherboarding to match existing siding. Apply a wood preservative to the exterior to protect weatherboarding. Replace ten lattice members on the south side of the bridge. Reinforce all chin braces on top chords and the attachment of these chin braces at the bottom. Remove and replace all sixteen floor beams to match originals. Install new cross bracing between new floor beams. Repair the crack in the east abutment. Remove and replace all wood decking in the approach structures with pressure-treated lumber. Place a concrete bollard at each end of the bridge. Provide for the repair of the fire alarm and sprinkler system. Also, the steel beams would be sand-blasted and painted with high-quality rust-inhibiting paint. The contract for this project was let in November 1997 for $162,998.

Howard's Bridge

Replace the metal roof. Replace three missing cross-bracing members at the ceiling beams. Secure all cross-bracing to beams at each connection. Replace missing weatherboarding and apply wood preservative to the exterior of the bridge. Replace damaged chord members. Replace six split lattice members. Replace fifteen pegs. Replace two chin braces. Secure all chin braces at the top chord. Attach each brace at the bottom with steel angles and bolts. Replace one floor beam. Secure all cross-bracing to the floor beams at each connection. Replace beams, flooring and treads at the southern approach. Construct a trench drain system to separate the wood structure from the earth fill. Remove earth from around the wood members at the north approach. Repair or replace damaged wood members and construct a trench drain system to separate the wood structure from the earth fill. The contract for this project was let in April 1997 for $125,840.

Stovall Mill Bridge

Consolidate termite-damaged areas of the truss with epoxy. Attach two cross timbers below the beams to each of the longitudinal floor beams with one-inch through bolts. Clean all earth from around floor beams. Replace 25 percent of floor beams. Remove earth from behind piers. Install new approaches using treated timbers and construction of new concrete approach abutments. Treat bridge for termites. The contract for this project was let in November 1997 for $89,107. Once the extent of termite damage was realized, additional money was allocated.

Poole's Mill Covered Bridge

Replace the existing metal roof. Secure all connections of cross-bracing members to beams. Install new board-and-batten siding for the entire bridge. Apply wood preservative to the exterior of the bridge to protect weatherboarding. Replace twelve lattice members. Replace twenty-five wood trunnels by over drilling of the existing holes and install oversized trunnels to create solid connections. Reinforce connections of all chin braces at the top chords. Attach all chin braces at the bottom. Repair a damaged chin brace. Replace damaged floor decking or treads. Replace broken floor beams to match originals. Replace broken cross-bracing members at ceiling beams. Replace broken floor joists to match originals. Construct a new concrete pier in the creek to support the bridge at mid-span and to remove an existing sag. Remove accumulated dirt between the existing sole plates atop the piers. Remove earth from around all wood structures at the approaches. Repair damaged wood members. Construct a trench drain system along the end of approach to separate bridge from earth. Place a concrete bollard at each end of the bridge. Provisions also would be made for new electrical service and lighting. Due to the added expense of adding a midstream pier, the contract for this bridge was $283,403. An adjoining park is now open.

Red Oak Creek Covered Bridge

Install a new metal roof. Replace missing or broken roof rafters. Replace thirteen ceiling beams. Replace all cross-bracing between ceiling beams. Replace missing weatherboarding. Apply wood preservative to the exterior of the bridge. Replace ten split lattice members to match the existing ones. Replace twelve members to match the existing ones. Replace twelve pegs. Reinforce the damaged bottom chord member with a steel plate. Add guard rails to chin braces to protect from vehicular damage. Replace eight floor beams. Provide for steel hangars for each beam, original and replacements. Replace ten cross-bracing members between floor beams. Provide for reinforcement at each connection. Install new height restrictors at each end of the bridge. A contract for $176,253 was awarded in November 1998.

Watson Mill Covered Bridge

Apply a wood preservative to the exterior of the bridge to protect weatherboarding. Add horizontal guard rails to the chin braces to protect from vehicular damage. Add steel rod cross-bracing the bottom of floor structure. Make provisions to jack the bridge from piers and replace the sole plates with steel beams. Modify the heel plates as required for proper support of the bottom truss chord. Excavate earth fill from behind the retaining wall, south approach, to relieve pressure on the wall. Remove earth from around wood structure at approaches. Replace damaged wood members. Construct a trench drain system along end of approach to protect structure from earth. Install new height restrictors at each end of the bridge to prevent oversized vehicles from reaching the bridge. The contract for this work was let in April 1997 for $165,880.

Ten Bridges Restored by Georgia Department of Transportation

Coheelee Creek Covered Bridge
Concord Covered Bridge
Cromer's Mill Covered Bridge
Elder's Mill Covered Bridge
Euharlee Creek Covered Bridge

Howard's Mill Covered Bridge
Poole's Mill Covered Bridge
Red Oak Mill Covered Bridge
Stovall Mill Covered Bridge
Watson's Mill Covered Bridge

Chapter 6

BRIDGE NUMBERING
AND PRESERVATION

B ridges through the decades have been given more than one name. The National Society for the Preservation of Covered Bridges has assigned letters and numbers to all covered bridges to avoid confusion. Pioneering bridge preservationist John Diehl developed the lettering/numbering system in the 1940s. According to NSPCB:

- The first set identifies the state.
- The middle two digits represent an alphabetical listing of the county.
- The next one or more characters can be numbers or letters. A number shows that the bridge is now or was initially supported by its wooden truss. Letters indicate that the bridge was initially built on steel beams or supported by something other than a truss. A capital letter indicates the bridge is large enough for a vehicle to drive through. A lowercase letter shows a smaller structure.
- Finally, if there is a # after the letter or number, the bridge is not the first covered bridge at this location. It could be the second (#2), third (#3), etc.
- Numbers ending with an *x* identify structures that no longer exist.

Here is a Georgia example in Bartow County for Euharlee Covered Bridge: GA/10-08-01. Another Bartow County bridge that is now lost: GA/10-08-03x. You see both bridges are from Georgia and in Bartow County. The third set shows these as supported by a wooden truss, and the *x* on the second label means it is a lost bridge—it no longer exists.[26]

PART II
THE SIXTEEN BRIDGES

EUHARLEE

Bartow County

Washington W. King and Jonathan Burke built this Town lattice truss bridge in 1886 for $1,300. Running 138 feet, the bridge spans Euharlee Creek.

33 Covered Bridge Road
Euharlee, Georgia 30120

Euharlee Creek Covered Bridge in Bartow County. *Courtesy of Vickie and David McEntire.*

Chapter 1

EUHARLEE CREEK
COVERED BRIDGE

S he laughs as she runs." That is what the Cherokees called the creek a few miles from Cartersville, in what was then called Cass County. Euharlee today is a tiny community with an impressive historic bridge in the renamed Bartow County. Euharlee sits in the shadow of Plant Bowen, spewing steam at different times night and day. A few small businesses and quaint shops exist alongside a handful of historic buildings, including the traveler's well that served the community and strangers. The centerpiece of the town is Euharlee Covered Bridge.

Initially, the area was called Burge's Mill after Nathaniel Burge (1790–1849), who settled in the county after purchasing eight hundred acres along Euharlee Creek and the Etowah River in 1837. As town commissioners, E.B. Presley, Leonard Morgan, Allen Dykes and B.D. Dykes incorporated Burge's Mill as Euharleyville on January 12, 1852.

Mount Paran Baptist Church and Euharlee Presbyterian Church opened the town's first school, Mount Paran Academy, in 1853. The name of the town was changed to Euharlee, and it was incorporated on September 16, 1870. The academy was renamed for the town. The school building burned in 1891 or 1892, but just four years later, a two-story building gave the academy a new home along with dorms for the students. This met the needs of students for the next eighteen years. It was not until 1914 that Bartow County took over the school and renamed it Bartow Rural High School.

Amid all this growth, Daniel Lowry came to Euharlee in 1864. He bought large tracts of land, as did his son, to farm and build a business. They had

Flour sacks from Lowry Mills at Euharlee Welcome Center & History Museum. *Author photo.*

a gristmill, a flour mill and a cotton gin. The mill generated electricity from the dam and supplied electricity for some of the community, a rarity at that time.

The remnants of that mill can still be seen alongside the covered bridge. The Euharlee Welcome Center & History Museum has a cotton bag display from Lowry's Mill. The Lowry family had property along Euharlee Creek for generations. The Lowry descendants either sold or donated their property to Euharlee. Many of the buildings remain, including the hand-dug traveler's well, a cowshed, the general store and a strange little building called a calaboose or jail. A calaboose is an outhouse-sized building used as a prisoner holding cell.

In 1886, the town hired Horace King to build a 138-foot Town lattice truss bridge over Euharlee Creek. This was not the first bridge; in fact, it was the third bridge. One of the bridges is said to have burned during the Civil War.

The foundation of the old Lowry Mill can still be seen near the north end of the Euharlee Covered Bridge. Builders made powerful stone piers with stones from Daniel Lowry's farm.[27]

After the Civil War and up through the early twentieth century, the population of the town dwindled. In 1970, it dipped to sixty-five. The town was rechartered in 1976. Washington W. King and John H. Burke built a sturdy Town lattice bridge that carried traffic until 1978. Georgia Power's Plant Bowen was built in 1976. During construction, building materials crossed the Euharlee Covered Bridge to reach the power plant site. Today,

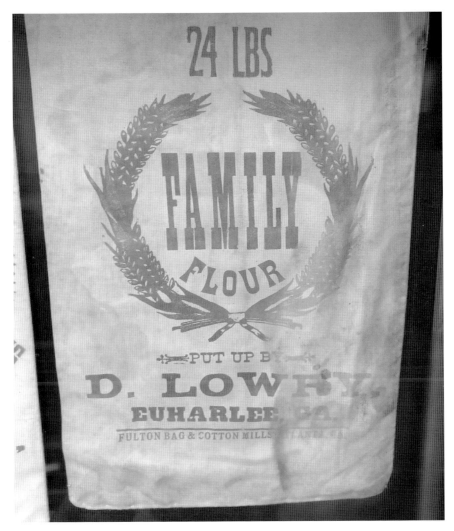

"Family Flour" put up by D. Lowry, Euharlee, Georgia. They made the cotton bag at Fulton Bag & Cotton Mills in Atlanta, Georgia. See my book *Lost Mills of Fulton County* for more information about this lost manufacturing business. *Author photo.*

the bridge is open only to foot traffic. In its time, the bridge provided transportation to the county seat and the commercial center in Cartersville. But this required another crossing over the Etowah River.

Today, you can visit this beautiful bridge at the end of the road at Euharlee. It sits parallel to its concrete replacement. The City of Euharlee maintains the historic buildings and artifacts in town. A spirit of preservation permeates this town. It allows the town to go on from one generation to another.

Euharlee Creek Covered Bridge in Bartow County is sometimes called Lowry because of the mills that sat to the left of this image. The ruins remain. *Courtesy of Vickie and David McEntire.*

Euharlee Creek Covered Bridge. *Courtesy of Vickie and David McEntire.*

According to the community development director for the City of Euharlee, the bridge has a built-in sprinkler system that was installed in the 1970s. She recounts a story told by the volunteer fire chief at Euharlee. Ernest Miller's son, who was stationed in North Carolina, called him and strangely asked, "Did the bridge burn down?" Someone had told him they had burned the bridge, so he called his father to investigate. The chief drove up to the bridge only to find that fuel had burned around the bridge, but the sprinkler system put out the fire. The Euharlee Covered Bridge was saved again for a reason. This town has many lives.

CONCORD

Cobb County

In the Concord Covered Bridge Historic District, this 131.7-foot-long bridge still carries traffic through the community over Nickajack Creek. A bridge has been in this location since the 1840s.

167 Concord Road SW
Smyrna, GA 30082

Concord Covered Bridge in Cobb County, winter 2023. *Courtesy of Lisa Miller.*

Chapter 2

CONCORD COVERED BRIDGE

Hiding in plain sight, surrounded by trees and with a creek running through it, the city of Smyrna is a place steeped in history. The water powered a nineteenth-century industrial park with a cotton mill, gristmills, a woolen mill and people who cared about their neighborhood. The industry has moved on and its ruins have crumbled, but what remains is a covered bridge and people who care about the past.

The Nickajack Creek runs under Concord Covered Bridge (once called Nickajack Covered Bridge) and twists and turns to build up energy that is used to power the mills down the creek. Some version of a bridge has spanned Nickajack Creek for decades. A covered bridge that sat to next Ruff's Mill was first built in 1848 and was burned by Sherman's invading army on July 4, 1864.

The current 132-foot bridge has more traffic than any surviving covered bridge in the state. This version was likely built in 1891 by John Wesley Ruff, who lived nearby and ran a mill.

Today, the Concord Covered Bridge is a key piece in the Concord Covered Bridge Historic District. The current district has these historic sites: the Concord Covered Bridge, Concord Woolen Mills, Ruff's Grist Mill, John Gann House, Henry Clay Ruff House, John W. Rice House and Martin Luker Ruff House. The Concord Covered Bridge Historic District provides self-guided walking tours from a downloadable app. I was lucky: I was given a personal tour by David, one of the homeowners and an active member of this group.

Left: Concord Covered Bridge in Cobb County, 1954. *Photograph from the Richard Sanders Allen Collection in the National Society for the Preservation of Covered Bridges.*

Below: Concord Covered Bridge before 1963. *www. concordcoveredbridge.org.*

David walked me down by the Nickajack, and we saw the famous Silver Comet Trail above us. He showed me some quirky places that might have been moonshine stills a long time ago. I got to stand by the bridge and watch metro Atlantans fight over who goes over the one-lane bridge first and how many cars can sneak by before the motorists on the other side start beeping for their turn—road rage on a covered bridge. As we crossed the street, David showed me the new guard rails that are replaced often. I am amazed this bridge still exists after reading about all the accidents that damaged it. A newspaper archive search will reveal all the accidents on the bridge with cars moving too fast or being impatient.

Concord Covered Bridge, 1970s postcard. *Author's collection.*

Concord Covered Bridge spans the Nickajack River in Cobb County, Georgia. *www. ConcordCoveredBridge.org.*

The Silver Comet over Nickajack Creek near Concord Covered Bridge in Cobb County. *Courtesy of Lisa Miller.*

We continued on our history tour and walked near the dam that had once powered all those mills. We looked at Ruff's gristmill and saw the Civil War pockmarks on the walls. A lovely couple lives in the miller's house. Standing near these buildings, surrounded by woods and with the creek making noise below, you feel transported in time. You can almost hear the mills working or even ancient gunfire echoing—maybe residual energy from the battle of Ruff's Mill. This book is not about the Civil War, but you can't avoid the topic in Georgia. For more on the battle at Ruff's Mill and recent archaeology, see the website www.concordcoveredbridge.org and explore more on your own.[28]

We walked along the trail and saw the Nickajack horseshoe. Part of the power of the creek is that bend. After what seemed like a long walk (it wasn't; it is my bad knees that exaggerate), we came upon the post–Civil War woolen mill, the Concord Woolen mill. There is so much to see in the Concord Covered Bridge Historic District, and it is worth a trip.

The historic preservationists around Ruff's Mill and the Concord Covered Bridge have done a remarkable job on their website telling the story, with Philip Ivester leading the way. I will borrow from them shamelessly but give them all the credit.

There has been a bridge at this location since 1840. At first, it was likely an open-deck design, and before that, people forded the Nickajack Creek underneath where the Silver Comet crossed overhead. This bridge is made of pine and oak. They installed a queen truss post to span the wider stream at Concord. They also placed two uprights across the span, and the result is a queen post.[29]

The bridge was used for transportation until 1973 and then closed until the 1990s for safety and traffic issues. It has the highest traffic count of all the covered bridges in the state. Steel beams were added to support the bridge and additional concrete piers in the 1950s. There is also a fourth all-steel support on the bridge. The Concord Covered Bridge has the distinction of being the only covered bridge still in use on a public highway in the metropolitan Atlanta area. The east–west connector was completed in December 1997, relieving most of the increasing traffic from the bridge and the historic district.

Over the years, the bridge has needed repairs and regular maintenance. Floods and other natural events damaged the bridge. Years of horse and wagon traffic wore it down. These days, the bridge is damaged from careless vehicular traffic, but a *Marietta Journal* article describes a November day in 1891: "Concord's new covered bridge is finished and painted. It is a very solid structure, of good material, and has the appearance of durability. JW Ruff is repairing, remodeling, and adding improvements to his house."

Five years later, the *Marietta Journal* recounted a remodeling day on February 27, 1896: "There is a good deal of activity observable at Concord just now. Mill and factory are making full time and the bridge here is being remodeled overhead and strengthened with new bents between the stone pillows. Mr Wielcher, of Cherokee, has charge of the work."

On February 14, 1963, the *Marietta Journal* described how the bridge was prepared for 1960s traffic:

The covered bridge, which dates back to at least 1890 and is probably older, is getting a new wood floor and stronger floor supports including two more concrete piers. Cliff White, the deputy county commissioner, said the Concord Road bridge work should be completed in two to three weeks. The covered bridge spans Nickajack Creek on Concord Road between Floyd Road and South Cobb Drive. County prison crews are strengthening the old structure by adding two concrete piers under it. In addition, steel beams are to be run the length of the bridge and this will be covered with a new wood floor. The bridge already has three supporting piers—one at each end and one in the middle, all built of stone. White said that to preserve the original appearance of the structure, he will enclose the new concrete piers in rock veneering. White said the additions will allow the old bridge to carry a maximum vehicle load of two to three tons. The present load limit is one ton. The bridge is one of only two covered bridges remaining in Cobb County. The second bridge is known *as Paper Mill Road Bridge east of Marietta. The cost of the two bridge repair projects is some $300k. Other roads provide access to both areas, White said.*

The *Marietta Journal* reported on March 11, 1963: "Concord Road was reopened to traffic last week after repairs were completed on an old covered bridge across Nickajack Creek. The floor was strengthened, and two additional concrete piers were placed under the structure to give it increased support."

In 1964, arsonists attempted to burn the Concord Covered Bridge and later destroyed the only other covered bridge in the county, Sope Creek. See this account from the *Marietta Journal* of February 4, 1964, of the attempt to burn Concord:

Arsonists scorch old, covered bridge. The old, covered bridge on Concord Road, a survivor of Sherman's vandals, almost bowed to a set of modern-day day ones Monday night. They tried to burn it twice and failed. A spokesman at the South Cobb No. 2 station said on the first try at about 8:30 pm only gasoline poured from end to end on the bridge burned. On the second attempt at about 12:30 am, a little of the wooden structure ignited. He said only minor damage was done. "It was mostly scorched," he said. According to Cliff White, Deputy County Commissioner, the bridge, built in 1862, underwent extensive repair work last year. "At that time," he said, "steel beams were put under it and a new wooden floor was added." The Concord Road bridge and the Sope Creek bridge are the only two covered bridges left in the county.

The next month, on March 30, 1964, the *Marietta Journal* reported, "The Sope Creek bridge was burned within two months of the attempt on the Concord Covered Bridge."

If the arsonists did not bring down the old bridge, the motorists would try. The *Marietta Journal* of April 22, 1965, reported:

County receives a check to repair the covered bridge. The Cobb County Commission has received a check for $596.04 to repair the famous Concord Road Covered Bridge which was damaged several weeks ago in an accident. A truck knocked out a panel at one end of the bridge—the only covered bridge in Cobb County—knocked rafters loose and bulged out the end of the bridge, which spans Nickajack Creek on Concord Road.

Commissioner Ernest Barrett said a Smyrna man driving a rental truck misjudged the bridge's clearance. The county now has a check from the man to repair the damage.

The bridge has survived and will thrive as the Concord Covered Bridge Historic District members continue to advocate for Ruff's Mill and the Concord Covered Bridge. Cobb County keeps the bridge in shape and safe. The citizens want the bridge to stay open, despite occasional bumps into it.

Philip Ivester, an invested member of the district, says of keeping the bridge open to traffic, "It takes you back in time. There's a lot of people who enjoy the historic nature of the bridge and the area. Occasional crashes into the beam is a small price to pay for the county to keep a historic treasure that means so much to so many."[30]

POOLE'S MILL

Forsyth County

Around 1820, Cherokee chief George Welch built a gristmill and open bridge. Later, a covered bridge was built and named for a local. It spans Settendown Creek. The original 110-foot bridge washed away in 1899. Bud Gentry rebuilt it in 1901 after a local carpenter botched the job.

7725 Poole's Mill Road
Cumming, GA 30040

The Cumming/Forsyth Historical Society has preserved Poole's Mill Covered Bridge. *Courtesy of Vickie and David McEntire.*

Chapter 3

POOLE'S MILL COVERED BRIDGE

Jimmy and Martha McConnell, co-presidents of the Historical Society of Coming/Forsyth, met me at the pavilion on the walk to Poole's Mill Bridge. Their walking tour helped me put this bridge in context, as they showed me the holes in the bridge. The original construction of this bridge began with a contractor who drilled all the holes in the lattice members in the wrong places. After fitting up the pieces, he realized they were wrong and abandoned the project.

Bud Gentry was hired to finish the work, but this required drilling new holes in the old members. You can still see the misplaced holes today. Because of the misplaced holes, Gentry prevented the treads of the bridge from being used. He arranged treads with holes side by side to be used in the chords, while those with diagonally offset holes would be lattice members. He pegged together planks at forty-five-degree angles and fastened at intersections. The bridge required 5,000 holes and 1,680 treenails (pegs) for every hundred feet.

Vell P. Fowler was the great-grandson of Dr. M.L. Pool, who ultimately hired Bud Gentry to finish the bridge in 1901. Vell remembered that Gentry's favorite food was frog legs, so Gentry gave Vell and his brother Jerrett ten cents apiece for each frog they caught for him.

We continued on our walk across the Town's lattice bridge spanning Settendown Creek (about ninety-five feet). This bridge replaced an original uncovered bridge built by Cherokee chief George Welch in the 1820s. Welch

Poole's Mill Covered Bridge in Forsyth County. *Courtesy of Vickie and David McEntire.*

Poole's Mill Town's lattice truss with a view of Settendown Creek. *Courtesy of Vickie and David McEntire.*

Poole's Mill Covered Bridge spanning Settendown Creek in Forsyth County. *Courtesy of Vickie and David McEntire.*

was a merchant who ran a gristmill in this location. He built his bridge using enslaved labor. The political atmosphere toward Native Americans was about to change Welch's life.

He had a trading stand built from his mill's lumber, and it was also a voting site for the old Cherokee Nation. The 1820s Indian Removal Act could not protect Welch. He lost his mill and home. He signed the New Echota Treaty in 1835 to prove his U.S. citizenship. A fraction of the Cherokees signed the treaty. The Cherokee removal was illegal, and it caused Cherokee leaders who did not sign the treaty to kill the treaty signers.

George Welch was a fugitive of his people. He wanted to stay close, so he moved to a land lot owned by his mother only one mile away. He was of mixed race and married a white woman, Margaret Jones. He may have faded into obscurity, but the mill he built ground meal for one hundred years after his death. The government appraised Welch's mill at $719.50 and the entire holdings at $1,250.[31]

I continued walking with Jimmy and Martha McConnell over the wooded area around the bridge and watched Settendown Creek. I complained about my bad knees, and we sat down by the creek. Jimmy walked down to the shoals and took a picture.

A stake remains on the banks of Settendown Creek. The stake was part of the mill. *Courtesy of Forsyth County Historical Society.*

According to Annette Bramblett:

> *Farmers grew corn and wheat and they had to be milled. The agrarian society needed gristmills. They used pulleys in their operation to enable the overshot water wheel to power both a gristmill and a sash-type sawmill. The structure was forty-five feet high, forty feet wide and sixty feet long. He* [George Welch] *built the tub mill on the banks of Settendown Creek. They built a dam and flume to divert the brunt of the waters to power the mills. In 1987, they backfilled the gristmill. All that remains of the flume are iron pins that held the headers of the flume in place.*

Jimmy had taken an image of one of those iron pins still in the ground.

In 1880, Dr. M.L. Pool (1825–1895) bought the mill. The area was renamed for the doctor, adding an *e*.

Bramblett continues the story: "A cotton gin was added in 1920 and was popular until cotton failed. The county turned to the poultry industry. Finally, the cotton mill was abandoned in 1947 and burned by vandals in 1959. The foundation remains and gives testimony to a long-gone way of life."

Poole's Mill Bridge collapsed in the 1980s into Settendown Creek. The county rescued bridges and shoals, converting the property from private property to county-owned, and created Poole's Mill Bridge Park. The park was dedicated on April 3, 1997.[32]

The Georgia Department of Transportation rehabilitated the covered bridge in 1998 as part of its restoration project. The Forsyth Historical Society recently painted the bridge to cover the graffiti. The bridge looked clean and beautiful as I sat with Jimmy and Martha on that sunny winter day.

LULA

Banks County

It was built in 1915 across Grove Creek and stands on original slab. It is on private property, and you can get a glimpse but not full view. It is a Howe truss bridge and is the smallest covered bridge in Georgia at only 34 feet. Formerly known as Blind Sallie.

Antioch Church Road off · GA Highway 51
Lula, GA 30554

Lula is a very short bridge. It was moved and reconstructed a few times and is no longer available to the public, as it is on private property. *This 1960s image was found on www. bridgehunters.com.*

Chapter 4

LULA COVERED BRIDGE

L ula has an unusual story for such a little bridge. At thirty-four feet, it is the smallest covered bridge in Georgia and maybe the country. The quirkiness does not end there. People in the area call Lula by other names, including Hyder and Blind Susie. Blind Susie was an old moonshiner who rocked on her porch all day during Prohibition. Stories are sketchy, but she was said to have hidden her product under her skirt on her porch in Hyder. This story may be a legend, or perhaps Susie was sitting near another bridge. Ed Garrison, a seventy-one-year-old resident, disputed this name, the story and even the existence of Blind Susie when he said, "I think that must be a made-up name. I don't know anything about no Blind Susie."

Garrison remembered when the Lula Covered Bridge was the primary route between Gillsville and Lula. Back in the day, it saw all sorts of traffic—school buses, farm animals and families—all making their way. He remembered, "Sometimes it was hard to get the horses and mules to get through it. They act crazy, run sideways and act skittish. Some of them walk through it like it's nothin', but others will try to act crazy and try to start up the wagon or buggy or whatever you have behind it."[33]

People consider Lula a lost bridge because of its shortness and elusiveness, making it inaccessible. This bridge's history is shifty. Some details are unclear, and the location is confusing. This is what we know.

In 1915, W.M. Thomas built a king rod truss over Grove Creek in Banks County that served until 1969. In 1975, the bridge was dismantled and its parts placed on the banks of the creek before being lifted by crane back to their original foundation. The strange thing is that the bridge has been taken apart several times. It is hard to keep the Lula history consistent. The *Gainesville Times* did a story in 2009 that adds some details but also adds more questions to the tangled web.

According to Rick Billingslea, a former Banks County Chamber member, in 2009 a group of Future Business Leaders of America (FBLA) students tried to restore the bridge to its early shingled siding. He said, "It was a project that was taken on, not without controversy, by the FBLA students as a community service project. The kids, with a couple of adults supervising, but mostly the kids, stripped the bridge down and got old pictures of it and restored back to what it looked like originally."

The bridge sits on private land on an abandoned golf course. The only access is a steep decline, and you have to cross two private property lines. Billingslea said, "Both property owners agreed to donate a piece of the property, but it has to be in the name of somebody....We also wanted to put in an access road with parking."

With all the complications, the project lost supporters. The students graduated, and the project just ended after the restoration. He said, "You had local people that would not support it because it was on private property.... They wanted the kids to get the title for the property before they started the renovation. Basically, it was such a monumental effort, and most of the kids involved with it graduated. It was supposed to be handed over to the historical society."[34]

At the date of this publication, Lula is difficult to get to or see, and it is not being maintained. A plaque was placed explaining a 1976 renovation:

> *Restored in 1976 by Bridge Builder Harry Holland is dedicated this day to the good people of Banks county for their use and enjoyment as a historical attraction thanks to the work an Generosity of*
> *Sam Rogers—Landowner*
> *Clint Tate—Landowner*
> *Milton Patterson—Banks County Commissioner*
> *Bonnie Johnson—Banks County Chamber of Commerce*
> *Andrew Walker—dedicated Friend*
> *Bill Jackson—Banks County Historical Society*
> *October 21, 1994*[35]

It's too bad no one can see this plaque. Maybe Lula will end up on the list of lost bridges of Georgia. History preservation matters even if you cannot see the location.

At one time, Banks County had thirteen covered bridges. A flood in the mid-1980s took them all out except Lula. I wonder what Blind Sallie is thinking as she rocks on her heavenly front porch; maybe she is the author of all this confusion.

HURRICANE SHOALS

Jackson County

Built over the North Oconee River in 1870, the 127-foot Town lattice design was burned in 1972. The Tumbling Waters Society obtained a federal grant, and the bridge was reconstructed in 2002.

416 Hurricane Shoals Road
Maysville, GA   30558

Hurricane Shoals Covered Bridge and the surrounding area have an interesting Native American legacy. *Image edited by the author.*

Chapter 5

HURRICANE SHOALS
COVERED BRIDGE

In an earlier time, this area was a Creek and Cherokee campground called Yamtrahoochee or Hurricane Shoals. The Native Americans believed that the Great Spirit once lived in a place between Tumbling Shoals (Yamacutah) and Hurricane Shoals. The Choctaw told early settlers that this land was neutral and no blood was to be shed here, not even for hunting. The pioneers violated that holy ground and then began a settlement. From early on, there seemed to be conflict. The Hurricane Shoals Park has a dedicated website with a great deal of historical information (www.hurricaneshoalspark.org/covered-bridge).

A 127-foot bridge was built over the Oconee on September 16, 1869. The bridge was in use by 1870 on a county road a short distance off Georgia's 82 Spur, about three miles south of Maysville and north of Jefferson. The bridge was a Town lattice truss—a popular Georgia design.

In 1906, Dr. L.G. Hardman, later governor of Georgia (1927–31), purchased the property. He opened a natural spring on the northeast side of the river to the public and named it for his sister Sally Hardman. Natural springs were big business in early Georgia history. Many false claims were made of their healing properties by legit and illegitimate doctors. Dr. Hardman may not have been this kind of doctor, but he was a businessman as much as a doctor. He built an electric generator to power his boomtown. In 1930, Georgia Power bought Hardman's property and operated the plant for two years before giving up on it.

Hurricane Shoals Park surrounding the covered bridge. *Adobe Stock, edited by the author.*

In 1962, four businessmen bought the property from Georgia Power. They saw the shoals as a future recreation facility. These men formed the Hurricane Shoals Park Association, but the area was not maintained. People were not invested in the area, and community volunteers hauled off eighteen dump truckloads of garbage. In 1963, they bypassed the covered bridge. Jackson County repaired it and built a park around it.

In 1973, Jackson County leased the land from Hurricane Shoals Park Association. That group rehabbed and cared for the area in the mid-1970s and opened it to the public as a county park. The county hired the caretaker, and the local 4-H invested. Additional acres were added during this time.

The county did not rebuild the covered bridge that burned on May 31, 1972, until 2000. You can see the original footings. This bridge was not part of GDOT's covered bridge restoration. Retired GDOT bridge engineer Paul Liles explains, "We didn't work on Hurricane Shoals Covered Bridge. They burned this one down around 1972. They rebuilt it using new construction after our project. Although the reconstruction used some GDOT funding, it was not part of the original repair and rehabilitation project."

This relationship is explained on the Hurricane Shoals historical marker:

In 1994, work began to secure federal and local funding to rebuild the bridge and to construct a historic village. Key players included the Tumbling Waters Society, the Hurricane Shoals Covered Bridge Committee, DOT board member and Commerce native Steve Reynolds, and state representative and county commissioner Pat Bell. Dr. Cecil Hammond, a retired UGA engineer, developed the first working drawings for the new bridge. An "ISTEA" grant from the Georgia Department of Transportation provided the bulk of the funding for the project, which also included bike paths and related improvements. Private donations and county funds also assisted. The work was completed under the leadership of the Jackson County Board of Commissioners, Harold Fletcher, chairman.

The organizations were successful in creating a historic and artsy park. I wonder what the Choctaw would think of their holy ground at Hurricane Shoals County Park and the work of the Tumbling Waters Society. *Yamtrahoochee! Yamacutah!*

WASHINGTON W. KING

DeKalb County

This is one of the few remaining bridges built by Washington King. In 1891, it was originally in Athens. In 1964, it was sold for one dollar and moved to Stone Mountain Park. The Town lattice bridge was originally 162 feet long and was shortened to 151 feet.

Covered Bridge Lane
Stone Mountain, GA 30083

Washington W. King Covered Bridge is in Stone Mountain Park in the shadow of the controversial Confederate carving on the side of the mountain. *Image by Warren Price from Adobe Stock.*

Chapter 6

WASHINGTON W. KING
COVERED BRIDGE

M iss Effie had quite a reputation in Athens. She had four brothels (none of which she owned) at 175 Elm Street that left a lasting impression on the college town. Sharing the stage was a covered bridge named in her honor from College Avenue to Hobson Avenue. The official name was the College Avenue Bridge or the Oconee River Bridge, but everyone called it Effie's Bridge for Effie T. Mathews.

Built over the Oconee River in 1891, this pine and cedar construction was 162 feet long. It flooded in 1908 and was rebuilt, but that would not be the last flood to threaten a bridge built by a King. Another flood threatened the bridge in 1911, and it was raised 8 feet.

With his father Horace's training and his own Atlanta business, Washington W. King came to Athens near the University of Georgia to build in Town truss fashion. He won the building contract with a bid of $2,470. In today's economy, that bid would equal about $81,656.57.

A flood came to town on January 28, 1963, and damaged the bridge, and it was closed to traffic. Instead of repairing the bridge, the Clark County commissioners sold the damaged covered bridge to the Stone Mountain Memorial Association for $1. The Clark County commissioners moved Effie's Bridge in three pieces over sixty miles to its new home on March 17, 1965, at a cost of $18,000. WSB-TV filmed a two-minute segment in grainy black-and-white images called "Covered Bridge Put in Place in Stone Mountain Park."

Washington W. King Covered Bridge. They renamed this Stone Mountain Park bridge for the original builder in the fall of 2022. *Image by Warren Price from Adobe Stock.*

A 1970s postcard of the bridge still called Stone Mountain Covered Bridge. In a 2022 ceremony, the bridge was renamed the Washington W. King Bridge in honor of the original builder. This bridge was originally in Athens. Though this bridge is historically significant, it was not eligible for the National Register of Historic Places because it has been moved. *Author's collection.*

The move cost the bridge 11 feet, as it was cut from 162 to 151 feet. It was placed over Stone Mountain Lake and leads to a picnic area on Indian Island. For a time, it was just called the Stone Mountain Covered Bridge. But times they are a-changing.

On September 21, 2022, the Stone Mountain authorities renamed the bridge for its builder, Washington W. King. During the ceremony, plaques were placed on both ends of the bridge. DeKalb County CEO Michael Thurmon spoke at the rededication ceremony. The Stone Mountain Memorial Association board sat alongside the descendants of the Horace King family, including Horace King, a UGA football player from the 1970s who later played for the Detroit Lions.[36]

Washington W. King, better known as W.W. King, built other covered bridges in Georgia, including Watson Mill Bridge and Euharlee Creek Covered Bridge. Many of his other bridges in Georgia didn't survive the passage of time and progress. He lost many of his bridges in Georgia not because of faulty construction but because they were replaced with more modern bridges.

This bridge story is full of irony. In the beginning, King was selected to build the bridge, according to the *Athens Weekly Banner* on November 25, 1890:

> *The contract for erecting the bridge over the Oconee has already been awarded to an Atlanta contractor, who is now selecting timber for the purpose. It will be a magnificent structure—one span reaching across the stream. It will be built to stand for years, and on the most improved plan....Every train is bringing stone for culverts, and work on them will be begun at once. The granite for this purpose comes from Stone Mountain.*[37]

The most glaring thing about this is that Stone Mountain Park was constructed to honor the Confederacy and King's father was born enslaved but purchased his own freedom. King and his father waited out the war in Columbus, trying to be neutral.

Miss Effie T. Matthews (1888–1966) was still around when they moved her bridge to DeKalb County. Her legend lives on in Athens, Georgia.

STOVALL MILL

White County

Built in 1895 by Will Pardue, the 36-foot covered bridge crosses the Chickamauga Creek and is near the remains of a dam. The dam and bridge are all that remain of a complex that included a gristmill, sawmill, shingle mill and other enterprises.

2617 GA-255
Sautee Nacoochee, GA 30571

Stovall Mill was once the location of a 1950s Hollywood movie. *Adobe Stock, edited by author.*

Chapter 7

STOVALL MILL COVERED BRIDGE

S tovall Mill is a movie star, and it has more than one stage name. The bridge near Helen, Georgia, in White County is sometimes called Sautee, Helen, Chickamauga or Nacoochee. The original bridge built by Fred Dover washed away in the early 1890s and Will Pardue rebuilt the present thirty-eight-foot structure. It was built using the queen post truss over Chickamauga Creek. According to French in *Covered Bridges of Georgia*:

The superstructure of Stovall Mill Bridge is a typical queen-post truss. This type of truss, which replaced the triangle at the peak of the kingpost with a horizontal crosspiece, allowed the clear span of the truss to be longer. Therefore, the builder could span creeks of greater widths. Timbers found in this covered bridge are the largest in the state. The bridge span is 36.8 feet with a clear span of 33 feet. The entire structure rests on two stone piers. The lower chord of this queen-post truss is hand-hewn timber 18 by 18 inches. The upper chord is 11 feet 10 inches long and has a section of 10 by 12 inches. The vertical members of the queen post which support the upper chord are 4 by 10 inches. The bridge is 11 feet 10 inches wide and has 2 by 10-inch boards which form the floor of the bridge.[38]

The bridge was placed alongside a saw and shingle mill complex. Dover sold the operation to miller Fred Stovall Sr. in 1917. A water turbine powered the gristmill, sawmill and shingle mill. All are gone now; only the remains of the dam are evident. The mill and dam washed away in 1964.[39]

Stovall Mill appeared in the 1951 movie *I'd Climb the Highest Mountain*, starring Susan Hayward and William Lundigan. *20th Century Fox Film, photo edited by the author from the movie.*

Corra Harris, a Georgia author, wrote *A Circuit Rider's Wife* in 1910. Hollywood made her semi-autobiographical novel into a movie, *I'd Climb the Highest Mountain*. Stovall Mill Covered Bridge was in the opening shots. *Photo edited by the author.*

Corra Harris was a Georgia author who wrote about her life as a preacher's wife in the North Georgia mountains in the early 1900s. Hollywood came calling in 1951 and turned Corra's book *Circuit Rider's Wife* into the movie *I'd Climb the Highest Mountain*. 20th Century Fox made the movie in Dawsonville, Georgia, but some scenes were filmed near Helen and in White County. Susan Hayward (Mary Elizabeth) marries her Methodist circuit-riding preacher, William Lundigan (William Thompson), in the opening scenes. They leave the church by horse and buggy and cross Stovall Mill Covered Bridge.[40]

The bridge was closed to traffic in 1998. Vandals have been out in force to make their marks all over the bridge. The bridge is currently owned by the White County Historical Society.

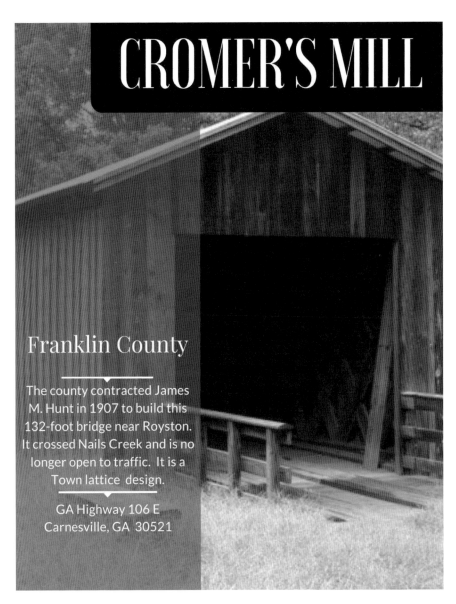

CROMER'S MILL

Franklin County

The county contracted James M. Hunt in 1907 to build this 132-foot bridge near Royston. It crossed Nails Creek and is no longer open to traffic. It is a Town lattice design.

GA Highway 106 E
Carnesville, GA 30521

Cromer's Mill in Franklin County is no longer open to traffic. *Photographed by David Seibert, March 15, 2001; image edited by the author.*

Chapter 8

CROMER'S MILL COVERED BRIDGE

C romer's Mill was named for a family who moved to Franklin County from Union, South Carolina, in 1845. The Cromers settled on Nails Creek and operated a woolen mill near this site. The community supported a cotton gin, flour mill and sawmill, though all ended by 1943.

J.M. "Pink" Hunt was taught by W.W. King how to build bridges. They completed the bridge in 1907 for $1,623. The Town lattice truss is of light construction, consisting of only three ten-inch top and bottom chords with seven chin posts for stabilizing each side. According to Thomas French, "The structure itself was constructed properly but poorly planned. The floor was built much too close to the waters of Nails Creek, and this has been the bridge's greatest problem. Attempts over the years to 'safe-up' the bridge are seen in the cables that hold this old structure on its low abutments."[41] Will Cromer, a descendant of the original family, built the stone abutments.[42]

Mr. and Mrs. W.H. Rice recall the community of the 1900s: "Back in 1903, there was a post office here and it [the town] was incorporated. The bridge was built in 1906 by [J.M. 'Pink' Hunt from Danielsville]. The lumber for it came from around down there too."[43]

Before the Depression, the community had a corn mill, cotton gin, shingle mill, wool mill and sawmill. Many a "Hoover cart" passed through that bridge on the way to get cornmeal. A Hoover cart was a cart pulled by a mule or horse, or it was built by taking the rear wheels off a car. It was a subtle protest against President Hoover, whom most blamed for the Great Depression.[44]

The Cromer's Mill community was once bustling in northeast Georgia. The *Carnesville Herald* reported that the people of the community proudly gathered at a little hill near the bridge to give political speeches.

On the dirt road between Carnesville and Athens, horse and wagon travelers had to stop and ford the shallow waters of Nails Creek in southern Franklin County until 1907, when the county built a one-lane covered bridge at the site. The area developed into a trading center with cotton, flour and sawmills. The town had a post office and a general store.

Eugene Phillips, a retired U.S. Army brigadier general, said, "In my grandfather's days, Cromer's Mill was a trading center and a community much like Royston is today. J.D. Baker had a store there with an amazing variety of merchandise. GA 106 has been rerouted to bypass the old community, but the bridge remains."

Edmund Johnson, in his book *The Bridge at Cromer's Mill: My Days of Sunshine*, leaves stories for his grandchildren. This is so important for the future, not just for Johnson's family but for everyone's history. Johnson's memories add to the narrative of the covered bridges of Georgia. Without these stories, we have holes in history and many falsehoods abound.

Johnson paints a picture of summer with cousins on the Cromer's Mill Covered Bridge. He said the little community was in a valley on both sides of Nails Creek. Tying the community together was the Cromer's Mill Covered Bridge. On the north side of the bridge were homes, the general store and an old mill. Farmers would bring their corn and wheat in for grinding into cornmeal and flour. The men in town would have horseshoe tournaments on Saturdays behind the old mill.

Johnson would explore the creek and fish and play on the bridge. The bridge had boards missing so they could see the water flowing. On the south side of the bridge was another store where the storekeeper and his family lived.

He explained that at the time of his childhood in the 1940s, there was still no electricity in Cromer's Mill, so the houses and stores used kerosene and oil lanterns at night. Johnson and his cousin watched a light show as the lantern light reflected on the creek. They decided to go to the store to investigate the light. In the store, moths trying to reach the flame surrounded the lamp, creating an ominous dance of light and dark. Men were sitting on Coca-Cola crates, and the light was bouncing and creating a mystical light show.

After that eerie experience, they crossed the bridge, and Johnson's cousin said, "They say this bridge is haunted." They started walking quicker until they were running to get out of the bridge as fast as they could. Johnson said the hair on the back of his neck did not go down until they got home. They never crossed that bridge at night again—unless they were in a car.

The bridge is still there, but the landscape has changed. Gone are the general stores and the mills. The community has disappeared, along with the post office. A neighboring property owner has limited public access to the bridge. One side of the bridge is on private property. You can only view the bridge from one side.

The Georgia Historical Society placed a marker in November 2000.[45]

ELDER'S MILL

Oconee County

Nathaniel Richardson built this 100-foot bridge, once located on Calls Creek, in 1897. John Chandler moved the bridge on a wagon in 1924 to its present location. It is now over Rose Creek and still carries traffic without steel support beams.

1441 Elder Mill Road
Watkinsville, GA 30677

Elder's Mill was moved from another location on a wagon over Rose Creek. *Photo and editing by the author.*

ELDER'S MILL COVERED BRIDGE

Elder's Mill was built in 1897 by Nathaniel and David Richardson. It has had many caretakers over the years, even when it moved away from its birthplace. It was originally built over Calls Creek on the Watkinsville-Athens Road, just north of Watkinsville, Georgia. John Chandler of Watkinsville dismantled it in 1924 and moved it to its present location. He put the bridge on a wagon and pulled it to Rose Creek. It used to be in the center of Oconee County. The county moved the bridge to protect it from increasing traffic. They chose the location over Rose Creek just upstream from a gristmill. The gristmill closed in 1941.

A local reporter shared this about his love for Elder's Mill Covered Bridge:

As a symbol of Oconee, Elder Mill Covered Bridge means different things to different people. Whether it's your family's tradition to ride through the bridge around Christmas while it's lit with bright multi-colored lights provided by the Watkinsville Garden Club and decorated by a local Boy Scout troop or it's a site of memories from picnics, Elder Mill Covered Bridge provides a chance to experience and celebrate Oconee.[46]

Reporter Adam Hammond covered the news of the bridge moving:

I'm grateful to the county's voters for renewing the SPLOST [A special-purpose local-option sales tax (SPLOST) is a financing method for funding capital outlay projects in Georgia. It is

Elder's Mill and Rose Creek. Al Cuming built a house next to the bridge and secured funding to save it from Governor Jimmy Carter. The locals called him the "Bridge Troll." *Author's collection.*

an optional 1 percent sales tax levied by any county for the purpose of funding the building of parks, schools, roads and other public facilities. The revenue generated cannot be used toward operating expenses or most maintenance projects.] *last November. As part of the SPLOST funds, $125,000 is earmarked for historic preservation. In addition to the work you're currently seeing on the Eagle Tavern's foundation, some of that money will go toward the conservation of Elder Mill Covered Bridge.*

Beginning next year, the covered bridge's beautiful walls and roof will receive new wooden pegs, and some of the timbers will be replaced. This effort and constant care of our historic structures will allow another generation of Oconee Countians to experience the unique stories and places that contribute to our community's history, identity and success.[47]

This ninety-nine-foot bridge is one of the last to allow traffic and is the only one that does so without steel beams undergirding it.

Elder was an unincorporated community in Oconee established in 1886 and remained in operation until 1904. A variant name was Goshen. Al Cuming's home sat right next to the Elder's Mill Bridge, and locals designated him the "Troll of Elder's Bridge." He retired to Oconee and found his paradise on a spot overlooking Elder's Mill Covered Bridge. He liked to think of himself as the caretaker of the bridge.

According to an article in the March 15, 1998 *Atlanta Journal Constitution*, "The bridge was in danger of collapsing into Rose Creek, so Cuming asked Governor Jimmy Carter for funds to stabilize it." He continued to find funding to restore and repair the bridge. At eighty, he was asked why he worked so hard to save the old covered bridge. He said, "I'm a Vermonter. 'Nuff said."[48]

Al Cuming died on January 15, 2015, and was remembered with a plaque at the Elder's Mill Covered Bridge. The *Oconee Enterprise* had many articles telling about the work of the Troll of Elder's Mill Covered Bridge. He had the bridge lit at Christmas with the help of the Boy Scouts and encouraged the community to care for the bridge. He lived in Oconee County for forty-five years.

Because of failing health, he had to move close to his family in South Carolina in his last days, but he made them promise to bring him back to the bridge and spread his ashes there when he died. They honored his wishes. In his own words, "'Nuff said."

WATSON MILL

Madison County

Washington King built this Town lattice truss in 1885. At 229 feet long, it is the longest covered bridge in the state and one of the longest in the U.S. Located in Watson Mill Bridge State Park, it spans the South Fork River.

650 Watson Mill Road
Comer, GA 30629

Watson Mill is in a Georgia state park and was at one time the center of an industrial mill area. *Author's collection.*

WATSON MILL COVERED BRIDGE

Washington "W.W." King built this bridge in 1885 over the south fork of the Broad River. Using superlatives for covered bridges can be lazy research and writing—just do a Google search for Georgia-covered bridges. But at 229 feet long, Watson Mill Bridge is the longest covered bridge in the state and one of the longest in the United States. The structure is supported by a Town lattice truss system and wooden pins. The approaches bring its length to 236 feet.

The superlatives continue as Watson Mill is also the tallest covered bridge in the state. King used double top and bottom chords in his bridges because of the length and the loads. You can still drive through this bridge upon entering Watson Mill Covered Bridge State Park. One more fact: this is the only three-span covered bridge in Georgia and one of only two line bridges that still exist.

King kept improving his construction skills. He had the weatherboarding dressed and added longer approaches to his bridges. He wood-planed the boards in such a way that water was repelled. Remember, in his day, there was no such thing as pressure-treated lumber. He had pride in his work and received the praise of county authorities. His extra professional touches added to the value of the finished bridge.

In all of King's bridges built after 1841, a numbering system was used to identify certain parts of the Town lattice truss. This would allow the builders to build quickly by using this numbering system to pre-cut and drill web members together. This speed allowed King to win more contracts because of his efficiency.

Watson Mill Covered Bridge spans the south fork of the Broad River on Watson Mill Road. The bridge sits on the border of Madison and Oglethorpe Counties. *LOC. HAER GA-140-8.*

Watson Mill Covered Bridge, February 2023. This side of the bridge is where the Black children would swim, while the white children swam on the other side. *Photo by the author.*

Watson Mill Covered Bridge is the longest bridge in Georgia, built in three spans. *Photo by the author.*

Some may ask why covered bridges have windows. It's dark in a long bridge like Watson Mill. The windows set on each side provide light for passage and a draft to keep bridge interiors dry.

In 1870 through 1890, the area around the bridge was not for recreation. The dam and falls generated power to run a flour mill, a corn mill, a wool factory, a wood shop and a cotton gin. A gristmill has been on the creek since the 1700s. Gabriel Watson was the owner of the gristmill in 1871, and the bridge was named for him. The area had a power plant, and the remains can be seen along the water's edge.

The bridge at first was not in a large state park but was part of a community for transportation and getting commodities to market—for commerce. But the bridge area has always been the place for social events such as square dances and even weddings. A turn-of-the-twentieth-century image shows lines of people standing on the rocks and shoals in front of the dam and the bridge. There are no bikinis; long skirts and long sleeves are the attire of choice. One thing the bridge area did not have was acreage, but that would change in the late 1960s.

Watson Mill Covered Bridge in reflection. *Courtesy of Vickie and David McEntire.*

Morris Marion Bryan's company donated land for Watson Mill State Park. *Photo by the author in February 2022.*

Morris Marion Bryan's (1889–1948) company, Jefferson Mills, Inc., donated 130 acres that allowed the park to grow in 1968. Jefferson founded the mills in 1916 and gained this property in 1932 for the company to produce power from the water from the dam. A stone with Bryan's image stands beside the bridge looking at the bridge and the amazing dam falls to recognize his company's contribution to helping the park grow. But that was not enough.

In the early 1990s, the state considered selling the park because of its size. But fate stepped in. The *Atlanta Constitution* reported in 1999 that a land deal for the state park increased the acreage by sixfold to the current size of Watson Mill Covered Bridge State Park.

The landowners could have made so much more money selling to developers. A Rome-based timber company could have harvested trees close to the bridge. A company wanted to place a convenience store a few yards from the bridge. "We had the opportunity to dispose of the land in other ways, but we'd rather see it as a park than an asphalt jungle," said Jere Ayers, a former state legislator whose family owned most of the land for four generations. It took seven years of negotiations to make the deal to expand the park.

The agent for the Georgia Department of Natural Resources in the negotiations was the Trust for Public Land, a national nonprofit organization dedicated to preserving historic sites and conserving and protecting natural lands. Landowners sold land to the trust and then gave the property to the state. The land deal was crucial to ensuring the park's future, as the park was previously too small at 144 acres. Now the park has over 1,000 acres to preserve and provide recreational opportunities.[49]

HOWARD'S MILL

Oglethorpe County

Named for a pioneer family and first built in 1804, it crosses Red Oak Creek. The bridge was rebuilt in 1905 by convict labor with the Town lattice design with lumber transported by the Smith and Dunlap Railroad.

Near Smithonia near Chandler Silver Road (County Route 311) at Smithonia Road

Howard's Mill is on a lonely dirt road just a few miles from civilization. The ramp has been removed, making bridge access difficult. *Author's collection.*

Chapter 11

HOWARD'S MILL COVERED BRIDGE

Howard's Mill is the saddest of all the bridges I researched. Once called Big Clouds Creek Covered Bridge, it is on the verge of being moved to the lost covered bridges list. It might have been the weather or the location, or it might have just been a long day, but something felt off about this place when I visited.

I followed my Google map to Watson Mill State Park and then went a short drive to Howard's Mill. I said short, not easy. The weather threatened all day as I visited other bridges in the area, but just as I hit a gravel and then a dirt road, it began pouring. I was not sure the picture I took was clear with all the rain, but the image provides at least a thousand words of what that place felt like. Going to places you write about is essential to getting the feel of the subject. I have to say, I got the feeling of Howard's Mill in a minute when I stood in the rain to snap a couple of pictures. I did not even get out my GoPro for some video. I wanted out of there—fast. I wanted out of the rain and out onto a paved road. The condition of the bridge is sad. You could not even get near it because the approach planks have been removed. Getting near to the inside of this bridge is impossible. The only way to get on that bridge is to jump, and I did not want to risk it. When I got home, I learned more about the community close to Howard's Mill Covered Bridge. It only added to my grave feelings about this place.

James M. "Pink" Hunt began construction in 1904 and completed it on March 5, 1905. Hunt was likely taught by Washington W. King in the Town lattice truss tradition. They made the 168-foot structure from heart pine from South Georgia that was shipped to Smithonia and then hauled over by James Monroe Smith's private railroad, the Smith and Dunlap Railroad,

Howard's Mill near Smithonia is no longer accessible. It may soon be on the list of lost bridges because of its condition. *Photo by the author, February 2023.*

just a few miles from the bridge site. The timber made the rest of the way by wagon. More on Mr. Smith later.

Howard's Mill Covered Bridge was named after settling near Big Clouds Creek in the late 1700s. Settlers established Oglethorpe County early in 1793. This was an ancient place in Georgia history. Some sources call this area Lexington, but others call it Smithonia.

On my way to Watson Mill Covered Bridge State Park, I sped by a town called Smithonia. I first thought it said Smithsonia (like the institute in Washington), and I thought, *Wow, that is interesting.* I had to learn more about that place. I did not like what I learned about Smithonia and its founder, James Smith.

Smithonia was once a bustling plantation, complete with a private railroad, Smith and Dunlap. The little town was close to Athens, Georgia. This historic community near Howard's Mill Bridge incorporated from August 23, 1905, until July 1, 1995. The town was named for Colonel James Monroe Smith (1839–1915), one of the three original councilmen and a large landowner.

At one point, Smith owned eighty thousand acres, making him one of the largest landowning farmers in America. On sixteen thousand acres in Madison and Oglethorpe Counties, he built an agricultural operation and created the community of Smithonia. The community grew with a post office, two rail lines, a hotel, a school, a commissary and, of course, his own mini mansion beside three enormous brick barns.[50]

In the post–Civil War economy, Smith nurtured a small farm into the state's largest plantation. At one time, he was considered the largest farmer in the country. He had political power as well. He helped put the Convict Labor Law into practice. Douglas A. Blackmon, in his book *Slavery by Another*

Name, exposed this horrible system that re-enslaved Black men by arresting them for minor crimes or no crime at all. Then, because Reconstruction Georgia was strapped for cash, businessmen and farmers could pay for the convicts to be released into their care and feeding. It was not a rehabilitation program; it was just another name for slavery. Smith was not only a user of the system, but he also helped put it into place as a state lawmaker.[51]

In his book, Blackmon explains how it worked in Smithonia:

> *If workers tried to flee, Smith relied on deputy sheriffs to recapture them and his own overseers to inflict brutal punishments. "They had dogs to trail them with so they always got caught, and then the whipping boss beat them almost to death," John Hill said. "It was awful to hear them hollering and begging for mercy. If they hollered 'Lord have mercy!' Marse Jim didn't hear them, but if they cried, 'Marse Jim have mercy!' then he made them stop the beating. He say, 'The Lord rule Heaven, but Jim Smith ruled the earth.'"[52]*

The convict labor worked on Smith's businesses on the farm. He had a sorghum, corn, timber and cotton mill on his place that was powered by this cheap labor. These convicts even worked on the construction of Howard's Mill. Smith's obituary in a random newspaper is recorded with his first name wrong: "Smithonia GA Dec 11. Joseph M. Smith, the most extensive landowner in Georgia died here today at the age of 70. Colonel Smith has spent many years on his large plantation in Oglethorpe County, adding to it from outside purchases as he could. He had built fertilizer plants, grist, and oil mills and other manu. plants."[53]

According to the Smithonia Farm website, Smith died in 1915, and his property was split up and had many owners and uses. The University of Georgia leased the brick barns for its equine breeding operation. Some of the acreage was sold, including eighteen tracts to the late Kenny Rogers in the 1980s. In 2000, Jewett Tucker bought the barns and surrounding acreage from Rogers. He converted the biggest barn into an event space. The land is now a venue run by Pam Shirah NeSmith.

Now, back to the bridge on that lonely road. In the 1960s, heavy traffic damaged and weakened one of the bridge's chords, and a support was needed. The bridge was added to the National Register of Historic Places on July 1, 1975.

I don't know; maybe it's my writer's need to find purpose and make sense of things. This bridge bothered me, and not for any rational reason. It's as if the bridge is in isolation. I think the darkness I felt when I visited Howard's Mill is related to the way those convicts were treated and the work they did on that bridge. Then again, maybe it was just the rain.

PARRISH MILL

Emanuel County

Located in George L. Smith State Park, this bridge was built by James M. Parrish, who, along with Alexander Hendricks, purchased the surrounding 200 acres from J.J. Moring in 1880 and set about building a dam and gristmill on Fifteen-Mile Creek.

371 George L. Smith State Park Road
Twin City, GA 30471

Parrish Mill is in the George L. Smith State Park. At one time, it housed a sawmill, a gristmill and even a cotton gin. *Author's collection.*

Chapter 12

PARRISH MILL COVERED BRIDGE

W hen I was on a weekend visit to my son's house in Louisville, Georgia, he asked me if I wanted to go see a covered bridge. I had just started researching this book and was not familiar with all the bridges in Georgia. It was time to get to know my first. He drove for what seemed like hours, and we ended up at a well-maintained state park. We parked, and immediately the sight of Parrish Mill overwhelmed me in the middle of George L. Smith State Park. This bridge site differed from any of the others in Georgia. The location was so unusual, with a pool of black water that reflected the exotic-looking cypress trees. The lawn was manicured and green. Most unusual were the mill and the covered bridge itself. Most covered bridges stand alone, but this was a combination of a gristmill and a cotton mill. This multipurpose mill can still grind corn for demonstration. This unusual place had an unconventional beginning.

In the spring of 1879, Alexander Hendricks stumbled on a two-hundred-acre tract with a small water source called Fifteen-Mile Creek. He felt it was a perfect place for a mill. The next spring, Hendricks and his partner, James M. Parrish, bought the land from J.J. Moring. First thing, they built a dam. The dam was dug by hand, probably using Irish immigrants and African American labor. A millpond formed, and they used a turbine-run sawmill to build the building. They built a covered bridge and drive-through mill around their sawmill, gristmill and small cotton gin. It might have been the first drive-through. The community could drop off raw products for processing and pick them up. People would bring in a cartload of cotton, and that small gin yielded about half of a bale.

Parrish Mills and Covered Bridge in George L. Smith State Park. *Author's collection.*

To construct a mill house, Hendricks and Parrish needed to convert local timber into board lumber. So they built a basic sawmill, most likely open-sided, until they had processed enough board lumber to enclose the mill. Once it was complete, the local community used the sawmill for building barns, houses and furniture.

The mill houses a series of individual floodgates that operate as a functioning dam, opening and closing as rising water warrants. This technology is primitive, but in 1880, it was efficient and reliable. The only modernization was an electric hoist to open and close the gates.

The mill used a turbine to convert water into usable energy. The turbine differed from a water wheel in that it created a "swirl" and could process more water by spinning faster. This component allowed the turbine to be much smaller than a water wheel of the same power.

The post and beam bridge/mill spans 101.3 feet across Fifteen-Mile Creek and was open to motor traffic until 1984.

Parrish Lake was created by damming up the creek. The lake fluctuates between 400 and 525 acres because of rainfall. The black water is a slow-moving channel that floods the woodlands, creating an almost swamp-like

Cypress trees coming out of Parrish Lake reflect green in the summer and red in the fall, 2022. *Photo by the author.*

A view from Parrish Covered Bridge overlooking Parrish Lake with the reflections of the tupelo and cypress trees, August 2022. *Photo by the author.*

A protected eastern indigo snake. Do not harm?! I am glad I saw the sign and not the real thing at Parrish Covered Bridge. *Photo by the author.*

Left: Parrish Mill produced grain until the 1980s. It is still a working gristmill that operates for demonstrations in George L. Smith State Park. *Photo by the author.*

Below: The multipurpose covered bridge over Parrish Lake and Fifteen-Mile Creek. More than a bridge, it was a sawmill, gristmill and small cotton gin—one of the original drive-throughs. *Photo by the author.*

Inside Parrish Mill, built in 1880. Samuel Russell, in the background, was built in 1996. *Photo by the author in August 2022.*

Part of the machinery in Parrish Mill Covered Bridge, August 2022. *Photo by the author.*

environment. As vegetation decays and the cypress become dormant in the winter, tannins leach into the water, creating an acidic dark-stained lake that reflects green leaves of the cypress in the summer and red in the fall. These trees can suck up four inches of water during a drought. Living in and around the dark waters are American alligators, eastern indigo snakes, gopher tortoises, great blue herons, white ibises and white egrets. The water is full of crappie, bream, redbreast sunfish and bass.

In 1945, Hubert Watson bought the gristmill and continued to grind corn and sell it across the South until 1973. Though the mill is called Watson Mill in honor of the last owner, it is confusing because the other state park that has a covered bridge is called Watson Mill.

When the mill closed, the state purchased the property in 1974, using heritage funds. Speaker of the Georgia House George L. Smith led the effort to preserve it as a state park. It was first known as Parrish Pond Recreation Area. The state legislature later renamed it for George L. Smith II (1912–1973).[54]

RED OAK MILL

Meriwether County

This bridge is the oldest in Georgia and the only bridge built by Horace King still standing. The main span bridges Red Oak Creek at 253 feet. The central span is 115 feet and is the longest unsupported span of wooden bridge in the state.

Covered Bridge Road
Woodbury, GA 30293

Red Oak Creek Covered Bridge. *By Jason for Adobe Stock, edited by the author.*

Chapter 13

RED OAK CREEK COVERED BRIDGE

Red Oak Covered Bridge is the oldest Georgia bridge still standing. No surprise, Horace King built it in the 1840s using the reliable Town lattice design with an approximate 2,500 wooden pegs. It is also a very long bridge at 391 feet, including the approaches.

Red Oak has an alias; some call it Imlac. Just like Stovall Covered Bridge, it has an IMDb credit. Television producers featured it in the 2012 bootlegging drama *Lawless*. It also has the notoriety of being the first covered bridge in Georgia to make it in the National Register of Historic Places (May 7, 1973).

Horace King's Red Oak Creek Covered Bridge is part of the National Covered Bridges Recording Project undertaken by the Historic American Engineering Record (HAER). HAER administers a long-range program to document historically significant engineering and industrial works in the United States. As remarkable as this longest and oldest bridge in Georgia is, it has issues. It gets wet.

Red Oak has been known to flood. Thomas French, in his book *Covered Bridges of Georgia*, shares this story of a local man's experience with the flooding bridge:

> *Mr. Frank Evans, relates to a time when he viewed the creek, eighteen inches above the floor boards of the bridge. He went on to say, "On another occasion a furniture truck once got stuck in the road on the south end of the bridge and the driver left it over night....He came back the next morning to pull it out of there....All he could see was the very top of that truck." The lay of the land around the bridge site is relatively flat with a very wide creek bottom.*[55]

Red Oak Covered Bridge, Woodbury, Meriwether County. *Courtesy of the LOC, HAER GA-138-13 (CT).*

Red Oak Creek Bridge, spanning (Big) Red Oak Creek, Huel Brown Road (Covered Bridge Road), Woodbury, Meriwether County, Georgia. *LOC, HAER GA-138-8.*

Red Oak Covered Bridge is the oldest covered bridge in Georgia and was likely built by Horace King. A new roof and broken pieces were replaced by GDOT in the late 1990s. *Image found at Georgia Historic Trust.*

During the flood of July 7, 1994, the water rose several feet inside the structure. Someone nailed a high-water mark metal sign to a truss.

It cost $176,253 to repair the bridge in March 1999. After the repairs, the east approach ramp was 252 feet, 7 inches long, and the west approach ramp is only 11 feet, 5 inches long. Counting the covered bridge length and both approach ramps, the bridge has a total length of 391 feet, 7 inches. Its tin roof was replaced with wood shingles during the repairs, along with most of the natural vertical boarding on the side and portals.

I dislike adding ghost stories to my books because we cannot use ghosts as reliable first-person accounts. But who does not like a good creepy story? A resident told columnist Bob Harrell this horrifying tale in 1973:

> *This tale has existed through all these years that in my father's lifetime there was a fellow (Hosey Spragins) who had a farm right up the road from my father's place. Hosey was driving home one night in his buggy after a trip to Woodbury. Hosey was rattling through Big Red Oak Bridge when he was hit by a body which was swinging from a rafter. The story goes that they hanged a man inside that bridge that day and left him there overnight. Anyway, Hosey was scared out of his wits and his horse ran away... preceded only by Hosey.[56]*

AUCHUMPKEE CREEK

Upson County

Herring and Alford Agency built this Town truss design in 1892. The original bridge spanned Auchumpkee Creek at 120 feet. Tropical Storm Alberto pushed the bridge 30 yards downstream in 1994. A New Hampshire covered bridge craftsman rebuilt the bridge shorter at 96 feet.

Allen Road, Highway 80
Thomaston, Georgia 30286

Auchumpkee Covered Bridge in Thomaston. *Photograph by Laura Clay Ballard, edited by the author.*

Chapter 14

AUCHUMPKEE CREEK
COVERED BRIDGE

The original Hootenville Bridge was built by Warren Jackson Alford and Dr. James Wiley Herring (1823–1911) in 1892 at a cost of $1,199. The bridge had a span of 96 feet between the stone piers and a total length of 120 feet, 9 inches. It spans the Auchumpkee Creek in the Hootenville Militia District of Upson County. The Thomaston bridge was renamed the difficult-to-pronounce *Auchumpkee*. Several other bridges were here before they built this one, and they had even more names, including Wilmont Bridge and Respess Bridge because they took their names from the owners of the nearby mill. Alford and Herring designed the bridge with a Town truss, where the 3-by-10-inch heart pine is crisscrossed and pinned at the joints with wooden pegs or treenails. This bridge was closed to vehicular traffic in 1985.[57]

The bridge was restored twice, the first time in 1985. On July 7, 1994, not long after the bridge's 100th birthday, Tropical Storm Albert dumped fifteen inches of rain onto the area in a single day and turned placid Auchumpkee Creek into a raging river. A huge tree limb was washed along like a battering ram and knocked the Auchumpkee Creek Bridge from its stacked stone moorings and smashed it against the overpass on Allen Road, thirty yards downstream.

With more than $200,000 in federal disaster relief money, the Upson County Commission and Historic Preservation Commission could hire one of the few abiding covered-bridge craftsmen in America, Arnold M. Graton of Ashland, New Hampshire, to re-create the bridge. Graton and his son

Auchumpkee Covered Bridge in Thomaston. Workers constructed the Auchumpkee Creek Covered Bridge, near Thomaston, Georgia, in 1898. It was listed in the National Register of Historic Places in 1975. It is a Town's lattice truss bridge. *Photograph by Laura Clay Ballard.*

Auchumpkee Covered Bridge under reconstruction. *Image found on Georgia Encyclopedia, courtesy of Thomaston-Upson Archives.*

J.R. headed up the restoration process of the bridge. The Gratons were experts in restoring old bridges. They used wooden pegs or treenails and huge beams put together in the original design. In 1997, they restored the bridge using pieces from the original construction. The cost of the rebuild was $209,000. The Auchumpkee Creek Covered Bridge, now ninety-six feet in length, was dedicated during the City of Thomaston's Covered Bridge Arts Festival, October 9–11, 1998.

This bridge was restored mostly with county funds and did not need repairs when the Georgia Department of Transportation was restoring bridges.

WEHADKEE CREEK

Troup County

Moved to this location in 2022 and rebuilt. Originally built by Horace King 1873 on Wehadkee Creek. A flood destroyed it and King's son rebuilt another in 1890. It was flooded and moved to Callaway Gardens in the 1960s. Returned home and is located in Memorial Park where King is buried.

101 W Mulberry St, LaGrange, Georgia 30240

The recently moved Wehadkee Creek Covered Bridge was returned to Troup County in 2022. *Courtesy of Lewis O. Powell IV, Troup County Archives.*

Chapter 15

WEHADKEE CREEK
COVERED BRIDGE

This bridge was first built by Horace King in 1873 over Wehadkee Creek in Troup County. The bridge's job was to carry traffic to Coalfield's mill. It had many names: Harmony Road Bridge, Neeley Bridge, Wehadkee Creek Bridge and then Callaway Gardens. It finally came back to its original name, Wehadkee Creek. In 1886, a flash flood destroyed the bridge. In 1890, Horace's son George built a 110-foot replacement. George moved their family business to LaGrange, Georgia, and renamed it King Brothers Company.

The Flood Control Act of 1962 for flood control, hydroelectric power, navigation, fish and wildlife development and general recreation created a man-made reservoir impounded by the West Point Dam on the Chattahoochee River. According to the U.S. Army Corps of Engineers, the lake has 525 miles of shoreline and runs for 35 miles along the river.[58]

James J. Keeble, a reporter for the *Columbus Ledger*, commented in 1968, "The last covered bridge in Troup County must either be wrecked or moved." Although the bridge had been abandoned for two years because a concrete bridge replaced the wooden structure, Troup County wanted to honor the history of the bridge. The backwaters would flood the area, but before the waters flowed and covered the bridge, someone stepped in. Callaway Gardens went to the Troup County Commission and said they would like to have a portion of this bridge at Callaway Gardens.

From the *Columbus Ledger* on September 6, 1965, we read: "The covered bridge that spanned Wehadkee Creek on the Harmony Church Road for

Above: Wehadkee Creek Covered Bridge was reconstructed after being returned from Callaway Gardens. Horace King originally built this bridge. It has returned home and sits beside King's grave in Troup County, Georgia. *Courtesy of Lewis O. Powell IV, Troup County Archives.*

Left: Wehadkee Creek Covered Bridge was named for the creek where it was first constructed. The bridge was reconstructed in 2022–23. *Courtesy of Lewis O. Powell IV, Troup County Archives.*

Opposite: The grave and memorial to Horace King sit beside the bridge he built, now returned to Troup County from Calloway Gardens. After his grave was found (he was lost for a time), a slab was placed for him and his son Marshall King at this site. *Courtesy of Lewis O. Powell IV, Troup County Archives.*

nearly 100 years was moved Thursday to Callaway Gardens where it is being restored for visitors to see the handiwork of artisans of the past." The bridge was a gift from the Troup County Commission. The terms of the deal were that Callaway Gardens move the bridge and place a marker telling its history. They placed it over a "diversion ditch in front of the Gardens greenhouse, according to a spokesman."

The article continues, "The bridge was moved to its new home on a tractor. Two giant cranes had lifted it from one side of the creek to the other. Each crane was capable of handling 50 tons. The trip to the Gardens was made with a permit from the State Highway Department at a rate of about 10 miles per hour." The estimated cost of moving and restoring was $10,000.[59]

Callaway Gardens moved a sixty-foot section of that bridge to the John A. Sibley Horticultural Center, and the bridge had a home there until 1983. Then someone at Callaway repurposed the bridge and moved it to a vacant field, where it sat decaying. The old bridge was unused and unseen by the public until 2021.

Meanwhile, back in Troup County, efforts were underway to find Horace King's grave. When the historical association discovered Horace next to his son Marshall, they placed two concrete stones marking the graves. (The marker had Horace's death year wrong, and efforts are underway to rectify this.)

Above: Home at last. Troup County refurbished this bridge and park to honor African Americans and King. *Courtesy of Lewis O. Powell IV, Troup County Archives.*

Left: The King memorial and his bridge were returned to Troup County with its original name, Wehadkee Creek Covered Bridge. Note the African American cemetery in the foreground. *Courtesy of Lewis O. Powell IV, Troup County Archives.*

Wehadkee Creek Covered Bridge was moved in the mid-1960s to Callaway Gardens. After a few years, it was moved to an empty field and closed to the public. The bridge was disassembled and returned to Troup County in 2022. *Photo by Jean Cyiaque of Georgia Department of Natural Resources.* Reflections *is the newsletter of the African American Historical Preservation Network.*

As part of the Mulberry Cemetery Renovation Project, the Wehadkee Covered Bridge was reclaimed from the empty field at Callaway Gardens and moved back to Troup County. The bridge crosses Oseligee Creek, connecting the Thread Trail to the cemetery. According to the *LaGrange News*, Callaway was thrilled to return the bridge to Troup County. "The Ida Cason Callaway Foundation (ICCF) Board of Trustees is delighted to be a part of the renovation of the Mulberry Street Cemetery by returning the King bridge to Troup County," said Fran Rogers, chairman of the ICCF Board, in a press release. "We are excited that many visitors in LaGrange will be exposed to the remarkable King family of builders."[60]

They returned the bridge to LaGrange on February 22, 2022. A YouTube video shows the bridge being transported back home and another as it is being reconstructed using original techniques, including the treenails in Town lattice.[61] The bridge is in view of the King graves, honoring the original builder.

Kathryn W. Tilley, president and CEO of Visit LaGrange, said of the day, "It is a great day for LaGrange, Troup County and our African American heritage. This would not have been possible without the partnership of the City of LaGrange, the Ida Cason Callaway Foundation, the Callaway Foundation, Inc., The Thread Trail, and Visit LaGrange, Inc. What an honor it was to witness the relocation of this bridge to LaGrange."[62]

COHEELEE CREEK

Early County

Built in 1891 for a cost of $490.41, it was restored in 1994 and had further improvements in 2014. This is the southernmost historic covered bridge in the U.S.

GA Highway 62 & Old River Road
Blakely, GA 31723

Coheelee Creek is the southernmost covered bridge in the country. It spans McDonald's Ford and Coheelee Creek with a series of unusual waterfalls. The gates protect the bridge from vandalism. *Image edited by the author.*

Chapter 16

COHEELEE CREEK COVERED BRIDGE

L ocated close to the Georgia-Alabama line is Coheelee Creek Covered Bridge, ten miles south of Blakely and in the Hilton community. Built in 1891, this structure is the southernmost covered bridge in the state and in the country.

Vandals have caused so much damage that a gate now restricts access to the inside of the ninety-six-foot-long two-span bridge across the Coheelee Creek. Built by J.W. Baughman with a king post truss for a labor cost of $490.41 with a crew of thirty-six, it took only four months to build.

The Historic Chattahoochee Commission and the Early County Historical Society erected the 1980s historic marker, which stated that the Early County Board of Commissioners had appointed a commission "to inquire into the practicability of construction of a bridge across Coheelee Creek at McDonald Ford. However, the construction contract was not let until July 7, 1891."

The historic marker continues to explain the area:

The Fannie Askew Williams Park, a picnic area adjacent to Coheelee Creek Covered Bridge on Old River Road, is maintained by the Early County Board of Commissioners. The land was made available to the county in 1959 by the late John H. Williams, of Blakely, and bears the name of his first wife. The Peter Early Chapter DAR serves as custodian of the park.

The Peter Early Chapter of the DAR was made custodian of the bridge in 1957. The Early County Board of Commissioners gave it preservation rights.

Imagine when there was no bridge to cross. Residents had to ford the creek, which could be dangerous in high-water situations. A bridge was a connection to commerce and a community.

In 2018, Hurricane Michael devastated the covered bridge. What cost $490.41 in 1891 took $150,000 to restore after the Category 5 hurricane dumped trees on the roof. Hurricane relief came from federal, state and local funds. Consider the cost of vandalism on top of the natural disasters. It is expensive to preserve these historic treasures.

The location is stunning and forested with a noisy creek below. The Coheelee Creek is a study all its own. Be sure to watch the YouTube series on Coheelee Creek. The narrator from Two Egg TV explains that the small waterfalls near the bridge are unusual because there are few waterfalls in South Georgia. The tiny waterfalls make a lot of noise and lead to a series of three more falls that end in the Chattahoochee River, the natural boundary of Georgia and Alabama.

Standing in the park, if you look closely, you can see across the creek and get lost in the trees and rocks. The YouTuber encourages visitors to go off the beaten path and find the bigger falls. There is an area where the water flows and seems to disappear. It looks almost like an infinity pool. The water cascades and rushes to two more falls down the creek. Finally, Coheelee Creek melts into the Chattahoochee.[63]

PART III

THE LOST BRIDGES
OF GEORGIA

Chapter 1

WHERE DID THEY GO?

F inding the lost covered bridges of Georgia is not easy. Thankfully, bridge lovers keep spreadsheets online. With the help of LostBridges. org, *World Guide to Covered Bridges* and the Georgia Department of Transportation for correct information salvaged, these lost relics can be remembered. Many early bridges failed or were flooded, so they had to be rebuilt with what remained of the lost bridge. Sometimes, residents just cut their losses and never rebuilt.

Georgia has always been saturated with water, both wild rivers and impassable streams and creeks. Just ask William Bartram, who traipsed through the well-watered areas of North Georgia in 1793. He described Georgia as "a body of excellent and fertile land, well-waters by innumerable rivers, creeks, and brooks." Rivers once defined Georgia's landscape. As the population swelled after the eighteenth century, people needed to move around. The Indian trails gave way to wider roads for wagons and people. Rocks and logs that forded crossings gave way to ferryboats. But early in the 1800s, innovators brought covered bridges to Georgia.

During the peak of the bridge-building era, Georgia had over 250 covered bridges dotting the forests. Communities grew up around these bridges that supplied transportation for milled grains and ginned cotton. These bridges provided mobility for Georgians, but their number dwindled to seventy-five, then twenty-five, to what remains today, in 2023: sixteen verifiable historic bridges. The reasons for the decline are many, but there are four primary categories that explain the demise of these wooden transportation tunnels.

Many covered bridges in Georgia were victims of arsonists and vandals. Some builders are to blame for shoddy construction. These bridges that were designed to last forever were subject to weather that hastened rot and decay. Bridges were easy targets for rising waters that flooded and even drowned some of these treasures. Sometimes, though, the bridge construction was so good that it was difficult to take them down when progress demanded it. From the data, I could find twelve bridges lost to arson, twelve to flood, eight that collapsed and eighteen that were replaced for progress. Hard facts are hard to find and confirm in this area of research, but with only fifty reasons accounted for, over two hundred bridges have disappeared without a trace.

Here are a few of the lost bridges and their documented stories.

Chapter 2

ARSONS AND VANDALS

KILGORE COVERED BRIDGE

Kilgore Covered Bridge was located in Barrow and Walton Counties. The community raised $300,000 in the 1970s to preserve it, but it was burned in 1993 by arsonists. The bridge spanned the Apalachee River on the Barrow-Walton County line.

Kilgore was built on site in 1874 by D.J. Thompson to replace an older bridge or ford. The land near the site was in the 1820 land lottery by Josiah Sanders and sold in 1823 to Joseph James, who had already settled on the

Ramsey's Photo Studio

THOMPSON COVERED BRIDGE
Near Gainesville, Ga. on the Chattahoochee River. In these dark tunnel-like bridges Murrell and gang, concealing themselves in the lofts, waylaid, robbed and sometimes murdered well-dressed strangers.

A lost Thompson covered bridge. *Courtesy of Bridgehunters.com.*

A 1930 photo of a covered bridge in Georgia with dirt roads and an old car. *Courtesy Digital Library of Georgia.*

property. An 1819 Walton County survey showed a private home on James Mill Road leading to the former bridge site. In November 1833, James deeded the property to Willis Kilgore Sr., who ran the mill for forty years and passed it to his son.

The land remained in the Kilgore family until 1889. Kilgore built a sawmill and gristmill near the bridge area that became known as Kilgore's Mill. The only remains of the dam are a sluice and some foundations. A third bridge, with two stone piers, was built in July 1894, and it survived until 1993.[64]

SOPE CREEK BRIDGE

Papermill Road or Sope Creek Bridge, with a 130-foot span across Sope Creek, was built around 1870. Cobb County still has a Sope Creek Mill community near Sandy Springs. The former bridge was on Papermill Road, but high school students burned it on March 29, 1964.

Sope Creek Covered Bridge, built in 1870 and destroyed in 1964. Historic American Buildings Survey, L.D. Andrew, photographer, August 6, 1936. *Photographed by Harold Bush-Brown. LOC. HABS GA,34-_____,1—1.*

Sope Creek Covered Bridge. *Courtesy Digital Library of Georgia.*

In Marietta, Sope Creek Paper Mill was a substantial mill covering both sides of the creek. Built in the 1850s, the Marietta paper mills produced paper products, possibly including the stock for Confederate money, which was of course destroyed by the invading Union army. Until 1940, the area was producing other things besides paper—flour, twine and electricity for one mile down the creek. An arsonist burned the covered bridge in 1964. The original stone piers are hidden beneath the modern bridge. The area ruins were added to the National Register of Historic Places in 1973.

THOMPSON'S

Before 1946, when arsonists burned it, this Hall County Town lattice truss bridge spanned the Chattahoochee River. According to the *Gainesville Times*:

> *Andrew Thompson built the bridge with his sons, Guilford and Ovid. They felled trees on the bluffs of Little River and floated them down to the Chattahoochee River to build the bridge. The covered bridge stood until 1946 when vandals set it afire. Andrew Thompson operated it as a toll bridge until it was sold to Hall County for $3,000 in 1898. It was the last toll bridge in Hall County.*

KNOX'S

This Hart/Oconee County bridge crossed the Tugaloo River. Colonel Samuel Knox built this Town lattice truss span in 1853. The *Greenville News* reported that enslaved labor built this bridge as a toll bridge in 1854 at a cost of $10,000. The architect was Colonel Bowman of Elberton, Georgia. Clark Mason was foreman of the work on one end and Judge Noah Looney at the other end. The *Keowee Courier* of Wednesday, March 11, 1908, reported that Hart County, Georgia, was refusing to help purchase the bridge. The owners sold the bridge to the government on April 6, 1908, and the tolls were removed. Oconee County, South Carolina, paid half and a group of business owners in Lavonia, Georgia, paid the other half. Hart County agreed to pay half of future repairs. In 1946, officials from both states announced they would remove and replace the bridge. They bypassed and closed the bridge to traffic in 1948. Its location is presently under Lake Hartwell. Arson was believed to be the cause of the fire that destroyed the bridge during the night of April 4, 1957.

PRAITHER'S MILL

This bridge between Georgia and South Carolina burned down. It was the last covered bridge to connect two states.

KEITH'S BRIDGE

This was said to be the longest bridge in the state but burned sometime between 1948 and 1949 during the planning of Lake Lanier. This bridge was between Hall and Forsyth Counties over the Chestatee River, which joins up with the Chattahoochee River near present-day Keith Bridge Road.

KESLER BRIDGE

This bridge, also called County Line, is in Urena, Banks County. It was built in 1925 and lost in the winter of 1980–81.

The bridge was named for the Kesler family, who lived in the area. At the formation of Banks County in December 1858 (from Franklin County and Habersham County), Kesler Bridge was mentioned as one of the coordinates for the new boundary. This bridge was reported as gone in March 1963. According to the Georgia DOT website, the weight of snow on the bridge caused it to collapse. However, covered bridge enthusiasts were still getting photos of it as late as 1970. One account says it went out in 1978, when a nearby landowner burned the bridge to end trespassing on his land. The bridge was included in a 1978 *Covered Bridge Topics* article about recently visited Georgia bridges. The fall 1981 *Topics* has a photo of the remains of the bridge, stating that it was lost during the winter of 1980–81. An article in the winter 1982 *Topics* stated that it collapsed and was washed away in 1979. The road was effectively bypassed by the construction of SR63 about one-quarter of a mile to the west. The 1951 Banks County Roadmap shows this crossing as a covered bridge. The queen truss was on the south end and the king truss on the north end.

WHITE OAK CREEK COVERED BRIDGE

White Oak Creek Covered Bridge in Meriwether County used the Long truss, which was designed and patented by Colonel Stephen Harriman Long. It was a single span of eighty feet. It was built in 1880 under the supervision of Horace King. It was well maintained by the county—until it was not. It was entered in the National Register of Historic Places on June 19, 1973. Someone burned it in 1985. This was the last surviving Long truss in Georgia.

Construction on the White Oak Covered Bridge was completed in 1880, and it burned in 1984. Seen here are the remains of the bridge in April 2013. The National Register of Historic Places included the White Oak Covered Bridge in 1973. *From Wikipedia.*

Roswell Covered Bridge

Roswell, Georgia, has quite a history (see this author's previous titles, *Lost Mill Towns of North Georgia* and *Lost Mills of Fulton County*, and in "The Others" chapter). This bridge always figures into the story. It was ultimately lost to progress, but its story goes back to the founding of the industrial town.

John (Jehu) Lowery built an original covered bridge in the 1850s, but the Confederate battalion burned it during the Civil War. General Kenner Garrard's Union cavalry arrived in Roswell in July 1864. Retreating Confederates burned the covered bridge at the Chattahoochee River, hoping to slow Union advancement. But Union troops crossed the waist-deep waters at the Shallow Ford (near today's river park on Azalea Drive). Charles Dunwoody built this second bridge in 1869.

The *Atlanta Constitution* carried a notice on March 28, 1900, announcing plans between the counties of Cobb and Fulton to build a new double-lane covered bridge of approximately six hundred feet to replace the old covered

This covered bridge in Roswell in 1910 is now a lost bridge. *Courtesy of the Atlanta History Center, 1702351.*

bridge that had stood for thirty-one years. Plans were to share the costs three-eighths for Cobb and five-eighths for Fulton, even though the boundary line for the counties was not quite in the bridge's vicinity. Piers were to be reused to the extent practicable; the old bridge was to be torn down in the summer and replaced. But it is unclear at present whether these plans went forward in 1900. The *Atlanta Constitution* of January 4, 1912, identified that a new covered bridge had been erected over the Chattahoochee near Roswell (presumably in 1911) at a cost of $6,180 to Fulton County. So plans in 1900 could have taken until 1911 to be completed. This third bridge stood until a concrete bridge replaced it as part of the Roosevelt Boulevard, Georgia Highway 9 connecting Roswell to Atlanta in 1925. The new bridge was named in memory of President Theodore Roosevelt, who often visited his mother's childhood home, Bulloch Hall.[65]

SHILOH

This bridge was in Banks County and crossed Hickory Level Creek. This Homer bridge burned in 1972 or 1973.

Chapter 3

ROT AND DECAY

New Salem

The New Salem Covered Bridge was built in 1938, a late date for a covered bridge, and did not have a long lifespan. It seemed to have been forgotten soon after it existed. This lost bridge, according to Thomas French, has little to no meaning to the residents of Banks County. To make things even more confusing and embarrassing, the State Department of Transportation records two dates of construction. From his research, French discovered the following from a front porch visit at a nearby home before the bridge collapsed into Gun Creek in 1983.

The bridge was built by the Honorable William Madison Thomas to replace the previous flat-top wooden-deck structure. Thomas was a farmer and a judge. He served as ordinary of Banks County beginning in 1935 and two years later became county commissioner until 1940. His side gig was building covered bridges, but maybe he should have stuck to politics, as evidenced by the collapse of the New Salem Covered Bridge.[66]

There is no evidence to suggest that Judge Thomas built any other Banks County failed structures. But you might wonder, considering his record. In Maysville, a bridge with three names—Perkins, Rylee or Twin Bridges—collapsed in 1970.

Earlier in 1963, another Banks County bridge collapsed. Hebron or Wright's Lower Bridge was not built by Thomas; it went up in 1915 by Herman Williams and went down forty-eight years later.

New Salem was the last covered bridge built on a public road in Georgia. The 1951 Banks County Roadmap shows this crossing as a covered bridge. The 1956 World Guide shows a 214-foot bridge half a mile south of SR59, perhaps corresponding to this location, though the length would have had to include approaches for this location. It was bypassed in 1967, and a culvert has replaced the crossing.

STEELE'S OR STEEL'S

This Cherokee County covered bridge spanned the Etowah River. It likely collapsed sometime after 1918.

The *Atlanta Constitution* of July 17, 1918, reported that Steels Bridge was a covered bridge. One truck of a military group being transported for maneuvers fell through the rickety bridge into the river on July 18, 1918, and there were casualties.

Chapter 4

FLOODING AND DROWNINGS

Eufaula Bridge

Eufaula Bridge, also named the Chattahoochee River Bridge or McDowell, was built by John Godwin and Horace King and was lost to flooding in 1841.

In 1837, a group of businessmen led by E.B. Young contracted with Horace King to build this bridge. The group of businessmen and King rebuilt the bridge after it was heavily damaged in the 1841 flood. Local citizens gathered the salvageable pieces to be used in reconstructing the bridge on its original piers. By 1847, the bridge had fallen down again, perhaps because of another flood or weathering. Apparently, the bridge was repaired significantly in 1849 and in the mid-1850s. The bridge was replaced in 1924 with a metal bridge.[67]

The Chattahoochee was brutal to bridges, even those built by master bridge builders John Godwin and Horace King. Though it was listed as burned at the end of the Civil War, the Dillingham Street Bridge (other names were Columbus or Lower) had flooding problems. This was the first bridge that John Godwin built in Alabama and Georgia. The contract was let to Godwin at a council meeting in March 1832. He began construction of the bridge in May and opened the bridge in September 1833. The bridge was lost during the Harrison Freshet, named after President William Henry Harrison, who had just taken office. It floated eight miles downstream before ending up in a cotton field. Godwin was contracted again to build the replacement bridge.

The contract for $15,000 for replacing the bridge was dated March 29, 1841. In August 1845, the bridge was unsafe and closed for repairs. Horace King also repaired it after it was damaged during the flood that took out the Fourteenth Street bridge. The bridge was burned in 1865 during the Civil War, and again King was contracted to build another bridge at the site in 1870.[68]

BROWN'S BRIDGE

The remains of Brown's covered bridge can be seen crossing the Chattahoochee River between Forsyth and Hall Counties. It was a Town lattice design with double top and bottom chords. This bridge was washed away in the flood of February 7, 1946. The floodwater carried its piers downstream, and they laid to rest on the Hall County bank. The bridge was essentially intact, which testifies to the excellent design and craftsmanship.

UNDER THE LAKES—LANIER AND ALLATOONA

During the 1950s, the U.S. Army Corps of Engineers were in a dam-building mode. And they lost things. In my book *Underwater Ghost Towns*, you can learn more about the U.S. Army Corps' mission and why bridges were lost under Allatoona Lake and Lake Lanier. From that book:

> *The Army Corps of Engineers improved navigation on U.S. waterways. They have served as part of the Army since the American Revolution. The Continental Congress organized the Army Corps to help General Washington's army. The Corps is still part of the U.S. Army.*[69]
>
> *The Corps of Engineers, named in 1802, had a larger mission between 1900 and the 1930s as the flood controller. The Corps had to benefit the national economy and include waterway navigation. While the Corps manage hundreds of multi-purpose dam projects today, they ambled along in 1918 with its first hydroelectric project at Muscle Shoals, Alabama. Thus began the big dam era for the Corps.*[70]
>
> *The Army Corps of Engineers and hydroelectric power helped usher in the New South. Government infused the agrarian economy with federal monies to build up the region beginning in the Depression through the buildup of*

World War II. The South Atlantic Division (SAD) of the U.S. Army Corps of Engineers has four major themes, according to The History of the South Atlantic Division of the U.S. Army Corps of Engineers, 1945–2011: *"Military Support, Civil Works, Environmental Protection and Restoration, and Management Leadership."*[71] *Mistakes were made along the way over the fifty plus years, but they always kept their mission of flood control, hydroelectric generation, and navigation in mind. Water supply and recreation grew in importance, but was not the original purpose of the reservoirs built by the Corps.*[72]

After the Army Corps of Engineers built and supplied the war effort and helped with post-war deconstruction of military installments, they returned to their first love of water control. Post-war Georgia, along with the rest of the Southeast, took baby steps toward environmental concerns and the Corps moved to a more balanced approach. Environmental issues and economic benefits were growing concerns of the people of the southeast. Increased water use and environmental impact became obvious in the 1960s and 1970s. No major construction in the South Atlantic Division has been planned for over 20 years. The Corps now focuses on maintenance and environmental restoration.

The U.S. Army Corps of Engineers began building dams and forming reservoirs in Georgia for navigation and flood control in the 1940s and 1950s. This began under the Flood Control Act of 1944 and the Watershed Protection and Flood Prevention Act of 1954.[73] *The reasons for the dams and lake have evolved. Lake Allatoona Dam and Lake was the first completed project in 1950. Followed by the Clark Hill project in 1953, later renamed for J. Strom Thurmond. Lake Sidney Lanier began and ended in 1957 with great pomp and circumstance. Lake Hartwell was filled with controversy in 1962. Carters Lake, the deepest Georgia lake, delivered the area of flooding in 1977. The Corps stopped building dams in 1985.*

Just as the Army Corps evolved from a navigation and building wing of the U.S. Army, the reservoir projects changed in scope and purpose. The History of the South Atlantic Division of the U.S. Army Corps *states, "No attention was paid to adverse effects to the land or fish and wildlife except as it involved a federally protected preserve."*[74] *They had specific objectives: flood control and regional development. "If archaeologists were needed to re-locate a cemetery," they hired it out. If a forestry evaluation was necessary due to proximity of a state or national park, the individual agency was contacted. At first, the Corps saw "little in-house need for such disciplines as biology, archaeology, or forestry."*[75]

Lost bridges have been discovered under our Georgia lakes. Helen Stell discovered a large piece of wood buried in the sand on the shore of Lake Lanier behind her home. It was not just any piece of driftwood. After doing her own investigation, she confirmed it was a piece that was part of the Browning Covered Bridge, which washed away in 1946. The bridge once spanned the Chattahoochee River east of Lula. Several bridges that were destroyed in the 1946 flood were replaced, but not Browning Bridge.

"It was a part of so many people's lives," said Stell after talking to Curtis and Ruth Cagle. She also talked to members of the White family, who lived near the bridge. Few cars used the bridge, which could be shaky for horses, wagons or people walking across. Before Curtis Cagle would cross the bridge to visit his grandmother, he would check to see if people had moved floor planks for fishing from the middle of the bridge at night.

In Bartow County, various bridges traversed the mighty Etowah River; all were lost to progress and replacement. One or two were torn down or remain at the bottom of Lake Allatoona.

Cartersville Bridge had an appropriate obituary by Depression-era writer Lucy Josephine Cunyus, whose Works Progress Administration (WPA) project left the county with valuable facts. Cunyus wrote, "The

West Georgia Underwater Archaeological Society found this 1838 Horace King bridge near West Point in Troup County. *Photograph by Laura Knight.*

Wilbur Kurtz took this photograph at the Stroup Iron Furnace, and in the distance was a covered bridge. The waters coming would flood both of these structures when they formed Allatoona Lake. These are drowned relics of the past. *Author's collection.*

old wooden bridge over the Etowah River, south of Cartersville, was built in 1883 at a cost of $3,477.20 by a Negro contractor, W.W. King." The *Atlanta Constitution* reported in 1927 that a new bridge was going to replace the Washington bridge.[76]

Most of the lakes of North Georgia would have had to demolish at least a bridge or two, including the infamous Lake Lanier. However, its less popular and far more interesting lake was Allatoona. Allatoona, unlike the other lakes of North Georgia, had actual towns underneath its waters, including Allatoona Pass and nearby Etowah. Pictures from the Wilbur Kurtz Collection taken while they prepared for the lake encroachments show one of the Stroup Iron Furnaces in the foreground and a covered bridge ready for collapse. The bridge was named Stamp Creek. (For more on the formation of the lakes in North Georgia, see my book *Underwater Ghost Towns of North Georgia.*)

I list these lost bridges on my interactive map "Bridge of Georgia." Go to the "Road Trip and the Purpose of Place" chapter for a QR code.

Chapter 5

PROGRESS IS A DAMNED THING

A Bridge Between Eatonton and Monticello

In a 1999 *Macon Telegraph* interview, seventy-nine-year-old Putnam County resident Lucille Green remembered in the 1980s when they tore down the covered bridge over the Little River near Willard. She cried and said, "It was on the road from Eatonton to Atlanta and when I was a little girl, we would go to grandma's in Covington that way. We'd sing on the way or stop and pick blackberries and plums. I loved that old bridge."[77]

This old bridge survived Sherman but did not survive progress. An article from 1938 said that the old route between Monticello and Eatonton was to be torn down and the steel salvaged for other bridges. The old route was abandoned as an alternative route, and a shiny new concrete bridge spanned the river. Covered bridges were deemed old-fashioned and useless. Even Sherman found the cotton mill nearby more useful to burn than this old bridge. This unnamed bridge was destroyed in the name of progress.

Jewelville

This bridge just disappeared. In 1951, a Banks County road map shows the Jewelville covered bridge. By the 1960s, it had been erased from the map.

A lost bridge near Eatonton, 1936. *LOC, photo by Carl Mydans E182.*

This bridge had other names, such as Strange Creek and Ragsdale Creek. By whatever name, it was replaced with a modern construction.

LEE & GORDON MILL

In extreme northwest Georgia, the Lee & Gordon Mill in Walker County that stood from 1880 to 1909 over the West Chickamauga Creek was replaced. According to the *Chattanooga Daily Times* of May 12, 1880:

> *Walker County has decided to build a new bridge across Chickamauga at J.M. Lee's Mill. We think it a very wise act on the part of those who have the disposition of such matters. It is to be a first-class covered bridge. The contract was given out at Lafayette, last Saturday, Mr. Hammond of Chattooga County, bid off the wood work at one thousand dollars. Mr. J.M. Lee is to furnish the lumber. Mr. J.M. Lee also took the contract for the rock work for one hundred and fifty dollars.*

The *Chattanooga News* on May 13, 1909, reported that the old covered bridge at the Lee & Gordon Mill was to be replaced with a steel bridge.

147

The lost Etowah Covered Bridge. This Bartow County covered bridge was near an old Stroup Iron Furnace; both were about to be covered up by the waters of Lake Allatoona. *Photo taken by Wilbur Kurtz, author's collection.*

GLASS BRIDGE

Some bridges just refused to go quietly. The King family construction company replaced Glass Bridge near West Point three times in the late nineteenth century. In 1956, they replaced it with concrete, making it the last major wood bridge over the Chattahoochee River. The concrete bridge was destroyed in 1973 as part of a reservoir project. A demolition team from Fort Benning used over two hundred pounds of C-4 explosives to collapse the bridge.[78]

WOOLLEY'S

Woolley's Covered Bridge was built before 1864 and spanned the Etowah River at 250 feet. The river destroyed it in 1886.

According to the Etowah Valley Historical Society, Woolley's was first known as a stagecoach stop on the route from Cassville to Rome at the plantation home of Andrew Feaster Woolley (1801–1865). He moved from

The lost bridge in "Etowa" crossing the Etowah River. This was not officially called the Etowah Covered Bridge; it may have been the Woolley's Bridge. *Author's collection.*

Fairfield District, South Carolina, to Cass County, now Bartow, in 1836, acquiring many tracts of land along the Etowah River.

After the completion in December 1849 of the Rome Railroad, which crossed the Woolley plantation, a railroad flag station was created at Woolley's. Originally chartered as the Memphis Branch Railroad and Steamboat Company, it connected steamboat traffic on the Coosa River in Rome with the Western and Atlantic Railroad at Kingston.

Woolley's Covered Bridge aided the Union forces' crossing when they found it intact. This site is along the old Rome Road, approximately two to three miles west of Kingston.

Service was stopped on the Rome Railroad in 1843, and the tracks were removed. Both the Woolley home and covered bridge no longer exist; however, bridge piers remain visible in the Etowah River. Two piers appear to exist, suggesting a three-span bridge.

PART IV

THE OTHER BRIDGES

They just aren't building covered bridges anymore—or are they?

At first, these two bridges were on my "sixteen" list: Haralson Mill (renamed Rockdale) Covered Bridge and Roswell. I realized that, though artfully crafted, the structures were not historic.

What makes a bridge historic and what makes it a reproduction? Most covered bridges were built in the United States between 1820 and 1900, with the highest concentration of construction being conducted between 1825 and 1875. According to the book of the National Society for the Preservation of Covered Bridges, *An Introduction to Covered Bridges*:

> *The term "historic" generally refers to those structures supported by wooden or mostly wooden trusses and built during the time when the use of wood was the most economical choice. That included most of the 19th century and, depending on the region, may have extended to as late as the 1950's. However, from the historic preservation standpoint, any structure over 50 years old is often referred to as "historic."*

A "modern" bridge that looks historic is a wood tunnel that borrows from the covered bridge–era designs using trusses. The techniques used during the covered bridge era that began in the early 1800s lasting until the early 1900s give credibility to these new structures. Traditional covered bridges were not, at first, reinforced with iron to support traffic. Today, this is required. This engineered wood is used today for heavy traffic.

The book *Introduction to Covered Bridges* states that "non-traditional" or "stringer" bridges were not built to be load-bearing and were supported with steel and concrete. According to the same book, "Some also use these terms to refer to historic bridges that have had steel beams or a concrete deck added underneath rendering the trusses non-functional." This book is arranged by the historic definition, even though some bridges had facelifts that rendered

ROSWELL

Fulton County

This is not a historic bridge but was built in the location of a covered bridge that was rebuilt after the Civil War. An original structure was burned by the Confederates in the mill village to prevent the Federals from crossing Vickery Creek. The pedestrian bridge over the creek connects the walking trail that begins in Old Mill Park to the Chattahoochee River trail system.

Vickery Creek Park Trail
Roswell, GA 30075

Above: Roswell Park Covered Bridge over Vickery Creek (Big Creek River). *By Marcus Jones for Adobe Stock, edited by the author.*

Opposite: Rockdale County Covered Bridge (formerly Haralson Mill Covered Bridge) in Conyers was constructed in 1997 to support the historic district. It is not a historic bridge. *Image by Leo Enrique for Adobe Stock.*

them closed to traffic. While a bridge might look like an "authentically built" covered bridge with spans supported by wood, others have a stricter definition. That is why Rockdale and Roswell fall into this category.

ROCKDALE COUNTY OR HARALSON MILL COVERED BRIDGE

Georgia's latest covered bridge isn't historic. In Conyers, Georgia, just outside but close enough to the metro Atlanta sprawl, is the first covered bridge to be constructed since the 1890s. It was built in 1997 in a historic district complete with an old general store, a blacksmith shop, a mill site and the Haralson Mill House. With the look and feel of an authentic covered bridge, this two-lane reaches across Mill Rock Creek.[79]

This 150-foot bridge was first designed as a pre-stressed concrete bridge. County planners made it a landmark, adding a large wooden superstructure and rock facing to the underlying concrete bridge. The lattice work is only decorative. The total cost of the bridge was $880,000. Concerned about the possibility of fire, they equipped this bridge with cameras, smoke detectors and a sprinkler system.

ROSWELL COVERED BRIDGE

Another covered bridge that is hard to categorize is the bridge over Vickery Creek in the historic industrial area in Roswell. This beautiful treasure, built in 2005, leads visitors across the significant waters that once powered three mills for decades to six miles of well-maintained walking trails. It gives a stunning view into the remnants of Roswell's textile past. Any Civil War history buff will appreciate the context, but this walking bridge is a smaller reproduction. I featured Roswell in two of my books, *The Lost Mill Towns of North Georgia* and *The Lost Mills of Fulton County*, to document its mill history.

STILL OTHERS

The aesthetic beauty inspires builders to add the covered bridge appeal to many subdivisions, municipal parks and resorts. Places like Big Canoe and Ellijay reproduce the look and feel of a time long past. While they can carry vehicular traffic, these bridges are not built in the authentic design of a bridge built in an era when they were vital for transportation and commerce. They just look good.

We use these bridges for decoration and usually just walking. Woodbridge Crossing or Arthur Max Bacon stretches across Nickajack Creek in Smyrna, Cobb County. Blackberry Mountain spans the Cartecay River southeast of Ellijay in Gilmer County, Georgia.

ROAD TRIP AND
THE PURPOSE OF PLACE

What good is a book about Georgia's beautiful covered bridges without directions? I embedded the following simplified map with an interactive map in Google's My Maps. Log on with the QR code.

Engage with the current bridges and the lost bridges. I designed a few trips so you can transfer the information to your own navigation system or phone. Remember, some bridges are on private property or border on private property. Travel and photograph with care.

Happy travels! Let me know how your trip went by posting on my Facebook or About page. (www.facebook.com/LostTowns or www.lisamrussell.net/about). Even better, subscribe to my Substack newsletter, and we can chat: lisamrussell.substack.com.

But before you go, there is one more thing. This is my shortest book so far. When I teach writing at the college level, the question always comes up, "How many words do you want us to write?" I have a different answer than most English teachers: draft a good thesis and support it with good words. I teach concise writing with clutter-removal techniques. Strict word counts encourage students to fill the space with unnecessary words. It goes against the way I teach and the way I write to add filler to meet a word count. I must be honest, when the words in this book were lower than in my other books, panic set in. Then I went back to the bridges of Georgia.

As I dove deep into the research that was scattered thinly here and there, discouragement set in. Where is the rest of the story? I looked everywhere

See where the existing covered bridges are and plan your own trip using this interactive map.

Find the lost covered bridges of Georgia on this interactive map. Close to two hundred have been located.

to find more stories and facts. With only sixteen surviving covered bridges, stories are scarce.

Then I discovered 250 or so lost bridges and sought to uncover their stories. But that brought even less information. Aside from standing on the banks imagining what was once there and comparing it to the few remaining images, their backstories were swept away with the years. I wrote everything I could find. Then I felt done. Like Tom Hanks in the movie *Forrest Gump*, "That's all I have to say about that." But after the dust settled on my frantic writing to the deadline, I saw one more thing. I saw the purpose in place.

Place is an abstract concept writers use to help their readers feel. Place is a character in any story—fiction or nonfiction. Writers want us to feel something, anything authentic. In a world that feels rootless, place connects us to deep-planted memories. We wrestle with artificial intelligence, fake news and confusing collapses of long-held truths. Everything seems turned around and upside down. Yet nothing is purer than place.

Visiting a covered bridge that once had a productive purpose invites us to imagine. Imagine a time when this was the only safe way to travel across wild rivers. In a less complicated world, fording a creek to get your cotton to market was essential travel. The covered bridge was security.

It might be painted over to cover sad, sadistic graffiti. It might have been rebuilt after it was burned down or washed away. It might have been moved from a different location, maybe even twice. Still, it is a solid structure and a metaphor for place. When you visit one of these bridges you can still walk through, do it in stillness.

Walk into the wood tunnel and away from the chaos of twenty-first-century noise. Put your phone on silent. Allow your mind to cruise in neutrality as you step into another time. Listen for the creaks and echoes as you cross. Look up at the magnificent architecture in trusses and siding. Look down at the roadbed that carried horses and wagons filled with product and produce. Look at the cracks in the floor revealing the rushing waters beneath—the point of the bridge: to cross difficult pathways.

The walk back opens your mind and gives you a new perspective on what is happening in your life now. Place is more than a backstory or setting; it is the character, the central figure that walks with you. Walk through to the other side. The walk through a covered bridge brings you to the other side with an experience. Something changes in your mind, from one side to the other. Coming out of the dark wood tunnel, you are different—even if just a little.

You have experienced the power of place.

GLOSSARY

abutment: A structure usually comprising concrete, stone or solid rock that supports the ends of the bridge at the shoreline.

bed timbers: Timber components are typically between the top of an abutment or pier and the underside of the truss bottom chord. Intended to serve as sacrificial components, they can be easily replaced when deteriorated from rot, thus protecting truss components from similar deterioration.

brace: A diagonal member in a truss slanting upward toward the center or midpoint of the truss, providing structural support.

bridge deck: The roadway through the bridge.

Burr arch truss: Theodore Burr of New York patented this truss in 1804. It incorporates reinforced arches that tie directly into the bridge abutment with a series of triangular support posts. It allowed bridges to span lengths over one hundred feet for the first time.

buttress: Timbers or iron rods placed along the outside of both sides of a bridge and connected to the ends of extended floor beams. The upper end was attached to the top of the truss-work.

chord: Horizontal upper and lower members that extend the entire length of the truss. The upper and lower longitudinal members extend the full length of the truss and carry the forces of tension and compression away from the center of the span.

dead load: The static load imposed by the weight of materials that make up the bridge structure.

deck: The floor or roadbed of the bridge.

flooring or decking: Planks resting on or secured to the floor beams that form the bridge floor.

floor joist: Timbers running across the bottom of the bridge supporting the floor planks. Sometimes referred to as deck beams.

floor stringer: If used, they span between the floor beams with the flooring or decking on top of them.

joist: Longitudinal timbers supporting the floor planks.

pier: A foundation support, typically made of concrete or stone, usually placed between trusses of multiple-truss bridges.

portal: The opening at either end of the bridge. Also, the boarded area of the bridge is at the opening under the roof. A general term for the entrance of a covered bridge.

post: The vertical or upright timber in a truss.

span: The length of a bridge between abutments or piers.

stringer: Longitudinal members supporting joists under the floor planking.

tension member: An engineering term for any timber or rod of a truss that is subjected to pull or stretch.

Town truss: Connecticut architect Ithiel Town patented his crisscrossed diagonals or lattice truss in 1820.

treenails: The wooden pins driven into the holes drilled into the plank members of a lattice truss to fasten them together. Treenails are also used to pin a mortised joint together. Some switch *trunnels* for *treenails*.

truss: A framework of beams usually connected in a series of triangles to support a roof or bridge. The overall assembly behaves as a single object. The triangular element in the truss is desirable because the triangle is inherently stable and resists deformation. A series of members forms a system of triangles to support each other and the passing loads on the bridge.

upper chord or top chord: The timbers running the top length of the truss.

upper lateral bracing: Cross bracing at the top of the trusses to resist excessive loads or wind pressure.

wingwalls: Stone or concrete extensions of the abutments leading away from the bridge at the far sides of the portals.

X (Long) truss: Colonel Stephen H. Long developed the X truss.

TRUSS DESIGNS DEFINED

The most basic truss design is the **king post**, which has been used since the Middle Ages. It is based on an equilateral triangle with a central post, known as the king post. The two diagonal timbers are braced on the ends of the lower chord and transmit loads from the center of the bridge toward the abutments. It is used for short bridges up to about forty feet in length.

The second basic design is called the **queen post**. The design has been used at least as far back as the Italian Renaissance. The queen post truss is an expansion of the king post design, adding a rectangular panel between the two triangles. It is often reinforced by placing vertical and diagonal timbers or rods in the open center panel. It was typically used to span distances up to seventy-five feet.

The **multiple king post** truss is an expansion of the king post design. The diagonal timbers carry the load from the center of the bridge outward to each successive vertical king post, which transfers it to the next diagonal timber. It is used for spans up to about one hundred feet long. Most have an even number of panels. With an odd number of panels, the center one may be open or have crossed braces.

Theodore **Burr** (1771–1822) was an inventor from Torrington, Connecticut, who patented his first bridge design in 1806. On April 4, 1817, he received another arch and truss bridge design patent. The patent drawing depicts a multiple king post truss resting on stone abutments, superimposed with an arch whose ends are seated against the abutments below the lower chords. Today, about one-quarter of the remaining historic covered bridges use this design.

Ithiel **Town** (1784–1844) was an architect who contributed significantly to the field of engineering when, in 1820, he patented a truss bridge comprising two layers of overlapping planks, forming a lattice fastened with wooden pins or treenails at each intersection. Town trusses were erected with sawn planks instead of heavy hewn timbers, making the timbers somewhat easier to work with. Town explained that it was "the most simple, permanent, and economical, both in erecting and repairing."

Colonel Stephen H. **Long** (1784–1864) became an army engineer in 1814. He undertook surveys for the U.S. Army Topographical Engineers of canals and led expeditions in the West. As a consulting engineer for the Baltimore and Ohio Railroad, Long became interested in designing and constructing bridges, patenting his Long truss design in 1830. A key to the design was driving wedges between the counterbraces and chords, which prestressed the structure and added substantially to its capacity. Very few Long truss bridges remain, primarily in Maine and New Hampshire.

William **Howe** (1803–1852) designed and patented the Howe truss in 1840. By substituting adjustable iron rods for the wooden posts of the Long truss, Howe's design was much stronger. He simplified erecting and repairing them, making the design well suited for railroads. In 1878, the American Society of Civil Engineers called it "the perfect wooden bridge ever built." Those in the eastern states typically have wooden diagonal braces in both directions, forming an *X*. Those in western states typically only have braces angled upward toward the center of the bridge. With an odd number of panels, the center may have braces in both directions and none. They found adaptations of the design in New Brunswick. Howe trusses became popular in parts of Europe, where some still stand in Austria, Germany and Switzerland.

For more details, see the National Society for the Preservation of Covered Bridges, Inc.

NATIONAL REGISTER
OF HISTORIC PLACES

T he National Register of Historic Places is the official list of the nation's historic places worthy of preservation. Authorized by the National Historic Preservation Act of 1966, the National Park Service's National Register of Historic Places is part of a national program to coordinate and support public and private efforts to identify, evaluate and protect America's historic and archaeological resources.[80]

The National Register of Historic Places has admitted several of Georgia's covered bridges, including some before they disappeared. It lists lost and current bridges with the year of their admission. Only nine bridges on this list remain. Some bridges do not qualify because they were moved from their original locations. For example, the Washington W. King Bridge was moved to Stone Mountain. Lula Bridge was moved one mile from its original location. The National Register of Historic Places listed Elder's Mill in 1994, despite its being moved.

Bridge Name	County	Year Added	Condition
Auchumpkee Creek	Upson	1975	Standing
Coheelee Creek	Early	1976	Standing
Concord	Cobb	1980	Standing
Cromer's Mill	Franklin	1976	Standing
Elder's Mill	Oconee	1994	Standing

Bridge Name	County	Year Added	Condition
Euharlee	Bartow	1974	Standing
Howard's	Oglethorpe	1975	Standing
Kesler	Homer	1975	Lost
Kilgore Mill	Walton-Barrow	1975	Lost
New Salem	Banks	1975	Lost
Poole's Mill	Forsyth	1975	Standing
Red Oak Creek	Meriwether	1973	Standing
Watson Mill	Oglethorpe	1991	Standing
White Oak Creek	Meriwether	1973	Lost

NOTES

Introduction

1. Larkin, "Philip Larkin, Bridge for the Living."
2. Firth, "Bridges Should Be Beautiful."

Part I

3. National Society for the Preservation of Covered Bridges, *Introductory Guide to Covered Bridges*, 2–5.
4. Ibid., 6.
5. French and French, *Covered Bridges of Georgia*, 8.
6. Ibid.
7. Most people do not know the lost story of the cotton gin. Whitney did not invent the cotton gin alone, even though his name is always associated with its invention. Not surprisingly, a woman, Whitney's boss, came up with the idea. See more at www.history.com/topics/inventions/cotton-gin-and-eli-whitney.
8. Lupold and French, *Bridging Deep South Rivers*.
9. French and French, *Covered Bridges of Georgia*, 10.
10. Lupold and French, *Bridging Deep South Rivers*.
11. Ibid.
12. Ibid.

13. Ibid.
14. Ibid.
15. King, "Testimony before Federal Commissioners on Claims."
16. CPI Inflation Calculator, www.officialdata.org/us/inflation/1859?amount=300.
17. King, "Testimony before Federal Commissioners on Claims."
18. *Atlanta Constitution*, May 13, 1883, 4.
19. Duncan, "King Deserves Remembrance," 37.
20. French and French, *Covered Bridges of Georgia*, 9.
21. Ibid.
22. National Society for the Preservation of Covered Bridges.
23. Ibid.
24. Liles, phone interview.
25. YouTube, "Restoring Georgia's Covered Bridges."
26. National Society for the Preservation of Covered Bridges, *Introductory Guide to Covered Bridges*.

Part II

27. Cunyus, *History of Bartow County*.
28. Ivester, "Covered Bridge."
29. Bogle, "Covered Bridge in Georgia," 8.
30. Croft, "Bridge Beam Hit 3 Times So Far in '23."
31. *No Protection*.
32. Bramblett, *Poole's Mill*.
33. Morales, "Outside Lula."
34. Ibid.
35. Martin, "Bridge Back from the Brink."
36. Bryant, "Bridge Built in Athens."
37. *Athens Weekly Banner*, "New Bridge."
38. French and French, *Covered Bridges of Georgia*, 54.
39. Garrison, "Bridges of Georgia Counties"; Georgia's Most Popular Recreational Travel and Events Guide, "Stovall Mill Covered Bridge."
40. IMDb, "I'd Climb the Highest Mountain (1951)."
41. French and French, *Covered Bridges of Georgia*, 34.
42. Bogle, "Covered Bridge in Georgia."
43. Ibid.
44. French and French, *Covered Bridges of Georgia*, 34.

45. Golden, "Covered Bridge Receives Status of Historical Marker"; Garrison, "Bridges of Georgia Counties."
46. Adam Hammond, "Elder Mill Covered Bridge Is a Treasure," *Oconee Enterprise* (Watkinsville, GA), n.d.
47. Ibid.
48. *Atlanta Journal and Constitution*, March 15, 1998, 64.
49. Osinski, "Magic Land of Mansions and Artist Colonies," 76.
50. Smithonia Farm, www.smithoniafarm.com.
51. PBS, *Slavery by Another Name*, www.pbs.org/show/slavery-another-name.
52. Blackmon, *Slavery by Another Name*.
53. *Enid Morning News*, "Noted Southern Planter Dies at Age of 70 Years," 1.
54. Moore, "Georgia's Hidden Treasures"; additional park information came from the displays at the mill.
55. French and French, *Covered Bridges of Georgia*, 39.
56. Harrell, *Atlanta Constitution*, August 9, 1973, 10.
57. Thomaston-Upson Chamber of Commerce, "Auchumpkee Creek Covered Bridge."
58. U.S. Army Corps of Engineers, "West Point Lake."
59. Orr, "Covered Bridge at New Location," 11.
60. Evans, "It's Coming Home."
61. WTVM, "Historic Bridge Returns to LaGrange."
62. WRBL, "Historic Covered Bridge Returns to Troup County."
63. Two Egg, "Coheelee Creek Falls."

Part III

64. French and French, *Covered Bridges of Georgia*, 51.
65. *Atlanta Constitution*, January 4, 1912; *Atlanta Constitution*, May 28, 1900, 9.
66. French and French, *Covered Bridges of Georgia*, 21–22.
67. Ibid., 12.
68. Ibid.
69. Bailey, "History of the South Atlantic Division."
70. Manganiello, *Southern Water*, 67.
71. Bailey, "History of the South Atlantic Division."
72. Ibid.
73. Ibid., 108.
74. Ibid.
75. Ibid.

76. *Atlanta Constitution*, May 29, 1927. Research notes of Thomas L. French Jr. as of April 1, 2015; Cunyus, *History of Bartow County*.
77. *Macon Telegraph*, July 11, 1999.
78. French and French, *Covered Bridges of Georgia*.

Part IV

79. Garrison, "Bridges of Georgia Counties."

National Register of Historic Places

80. U.S. National Park Service, "What Is the National Register of Historic Places?"

BIBLIOGRAPHY

Athens Weekly Banner. "The New Bridge." November 25, 1890.

Atlanta Constitution. May 13, 1883, 4.

Bailey, Ralph, Jr., et al. "The History of the South Atlantic Division of the US Army Corps of Engineers, 1945–2011." South Atlantic Division, U.S. Army Corps of Engineers. Last modified 2012. www.sad.usace.army.mil/Portals/60/docs/history/SAD_History_small.pdf.

Barker, James C., and James A. Barker. *Covered Bridges and the Birth of American Engineering*. Washington, D.C.: National Park Service, 2015.

Blackmon, Douglas A. *Slavery by Another Name: The Re-Enslavement of Black Americans from the Civil War to World War II*. New York: Anchor, 2009.

Bogle, James G. "Covered Bridge in Georgia." *Atlanta Historical Society* 27, no. 1 (Spring 1983): 5–28.

Bramblett, Annette. "Poole's Mill." Historical Society of Forsyth County, n.d.

Bryant, Tim. "Bridge Built in Athens Is Renamed and Dedicated in Stone Mountain." WGAU. Last modified September 20, 2022. www.wgauradio.com/news/local/bridge-built-athens-is-renamed-dedicated-stone-mountain/3IW7BDAZ2RCOXPZFZ6RACMT7UA.

Byers, Jeremy. "The Hauntings at Poole's Mill Covered Bridge." Horror. Last modified 2020. vocal.media/horror/the-hauntings-at-poole-s-mill-covered-bridge.

Byrne, Shannon. "An Uncrowned King: Uncovering the Bridges of W.W. King." I Am the Mountain. Last modified May 30, 2018. iamthemountain.org/2018/05/30/an-uncrowned-king-uncovering-the-bridges-of-w-w-king.

Carey, Anthony G., and Historic C. Commission. "Introduction." In *Sold Down the River: Slavery in the Lower Chattahoochee Valley of Alabama and Georgia*, 2–13. Tuscaloosa: University of Alabama Press, 2011.

Caswell, William S., and Dan Brock, eds. *World Guide to Covered Bridges*. 8th ed. Concord, NH: Quality Press, 2021. www.coveredbridgesociety.org.

Chandler, Dena. "Watson Mill Bridge Built by Son of Slave That Was Pioneer of Covered Bridge Building." Flagpole (Athens), n.d.

Covered Spans of Yesteryear. "Lost Bridges of Georgia." www.lostbridges.org/details.aspx?id=GA/10-03-01x&loc=n.

Cox, Dale. "Coheelee Creek Covered Bridge." YouTube. www.youtube.com/watch?v=UN_hpCFooZ4.

Croft, Taylor. "Bridge Beam Hit 3 Times So Far in '23." *Atlanta Constitution*, February 10, 2023, A4.

Cunyus, Lucy J. *The History of Bartow County, Formerly Cass.* WPA Writers' Project, 1933.

Duncan, Priscilla B. "King Deserves Remembrance." *Ledger-Enquirer* (Columbus, GA), February 19, 1988, 37.

Elliott, Daniel T., Philip Ivester and Rita F. Elliott. *Archeological Search for Ruff's Mill Battlefield: Linchpin in Atlanta's Fall.* Savannah: Lamar Institute, 2022.

Elliott, Rita. "Double Quick and Bayonets Fixed." YouTube. April 29, 2022. www.youtube.com/watch?v=z-TRea0-BGE.

Enid [OK] Morning News. "Noted Southern Planter Dies at Age of 70 Years." December 12, 1915, 1.

Evans, Daniel. "It's Coming Home: King Bridge Returning to LaGrange for First Time in 56 Years." *LaGrange Daily News*, March 31, 2021. www.lagrangenews.com/2021/03/31/its-coming-home-king-bridge-returning-to-lagrange-for-first-time-in-56-years.

Facebook. "The Covered Bridge Experience." www.facebook.com/groups/TheCoveredBridgeExperience.

Fincher, Cheryl. "Bridge to the Past." *Macon [GA] Telegraph*, July 11, 1999, 54.

Firth, Ian. "Bridges Should Be Beautiful." YouTube. July 18, 2018. www.youtube.com/watch?v=dKq34EVggjI.

French, Thomas L., and Edward L. French. *Covered Bridges of Georgia.* N.p., 1984.

Galloway, Jim. "With Truth Telling We Can Build Bridges." *Atlanta Constitution*, September 21, 2022, A13.

Garrison, Judy. "The Bridges of Georgia Counties: The Rich History & Last Remaining Covered Bridges in Georgia." North Georgia Living.

Last modified September 19, 2021. northgeorgialiving.com/the-bridges-of-georgia-counties-the-rich-history-last-remaining-covered-bridges-in-georgia.

"Ga.'s Covered Bridge Rehabilitations." Ted Cashin's. Last modified November 8, 2000. igirder.com/covered/istea.htm.

Georgia Covered Bridges: Auchumpkee Creek Bridge. www.gribblenation.com/gapics/covdbrdg/auchumpkee.html.

Georgia's Most Popular Recreational Travel and Events Guide. "Lula Covered Bridge." Last modified April 12, 2020. www.n-georgia.com/lula-bridge.htm.

———. "Stovall Mill Covered Bridge, Helen Georgia." www.n-georgia.com/stovall-mill-bridge.htm.

Georgia's Romantic Bridges. Georgia Department of Transportation, n.d.

Georgia State Highway Department, Public Information Office. *Relics of the Road: The Covered Bridges of Georgia.* 1965.

Gibbons, Faye. *Horace King: Bridges to Freedom.* St. Louis: Turtleback, 2002.

Golden, Nathan. "Covered Bridge Receives Status of Historical Marker." *Anderson [SC] Independent Mail,* November 4, 2020, 12.

Hagler, Laura. "Auchumpkee Creek Bridge." C-SPAN.org, June 23, 1998. www.c-span.org/video/?107840-1/auchumpkee-creek-bridge.

Hall, B.M., and M.R. Hall. "Third Report on the Water Powers of Georgia." Geological Survey of Georgia, 1975.

Hammack, Aubrey. "Rebuilding Auchumpkee Covered Bridge." *Georgia Backroads* (Spring 2009).

Harrell, Bob. *Atlanta Constitution,* August 9, 1973, 10.

———. "Covered Bridges Tell of Meriwether's Past for Those Who Listen." *Atlanta Constitution,* January 21, 1985, 53.

Harrison, Thomas. *Of Bridges: A Poetic and Philosophical Account.* Chicago: University of Chicago Press, 2021.

Hurricane Shoals. "Our History." www.hurricaneshoalspark.org/our-history-x5j5n.

IMDb. "I'd Climb the Highest Mountain (1951)." Last modified February 17, 1951. www.imdb.com/title/tt0043667.

Ivester, Philip. "The Covered Bridge." Concord Covered Bridge Historic District. Last modified February 10, 2019. concordcoveredbridge.org/the-covered-bridge.

Johnson, Ansley. "Historic Coheelee Creek Bridge." *Georgia Backroads* (Fall 2006).

Johnson, Edmund R. *The Bridge at Cromer's Mill: My Days of Sunshine.* N.p.: Archway Publishing, 2015.

Keeble, James J. "Waters Threaten Covered Bridge." *Columbus [GA] Ledger*, July 7, 1968, 68–69.

King, Horace. "Testimony before Federal Commissioners on Claims." February 1878.

Kissin' Bridges: A Practical Guide to Finding Covered Bridges throughout the State of Georgia. Alpharetta, GA: Byways Publications, 1990.

Knox, Shawn M. "The Eleventh Hour of Watson Mill Covered Bridge." *Georgia Backroads* (Spring 2003).

Kovarich, Joseph. *Vanishing Landmarks of Georgia: Gristmills and Covered Bridges*. Durham, NC: Blair, 2016.

Larkin, Philip. "Philip Larkin, Bridge for the Living." RihlaJourney. Last modified November 29, 2008. rihlajourney.wordpress.com/2008/11/04/philip-larkin-bridge-for-the-living.

Liles, Paul, Jr. Phone interview, May 11, 2022.

Lupold, John S., and Thomas L. French. *Bridging Deep South Rivers: The Life and Legend of Horace King*. Athens: University of Georgia Press, 2019.

Macon [GA] Telegraph, February 18, 1938, 3; July 11, 1999.

Manganiello, Christopher J. *Southern Water, Southern Power: How the Politics of Cheap Energy and Water Scarcity Shaped a Region*. Chapel Hill: University of North Carolina Press, 2015.

Martin, Sarah Hines. "Bridge Back from the Brink." *North Georgia Journal* (Summer 1997).

Mitchell, Louise M. "Memories of Past Era Rapidly Disappearing." *Columbus [GA] Ledger*, March 9, 1941.

Moore, Jovita. "Georgia's Hidden Treasures on 11 Alive." YouTube. April 13, 2011. www.youtube.com/watch?v=WlmPlcQ8NNc.

Morales, Kristen. "Outside Lula, a Covered Bridge Claims a Colorful Past." *Gainesville [GA] Times*, October 18, 2009. www.gainesvilletimes.com/life/outside-lula-a-covered-bridge-claims-a-colorful-past.

National Society for the Preservation of Covered Bridges. Last modified April 2022. www.coveredbridgesociety.org/aboutus.html.

———. *An Introductory Guide to Covered Bridges*. Concord, NH: Quality Press, 2022.

No Protection. Forsyth County: National Park Service: Trail of Tears Association, n.d.

NPGallery Search. "NPGallery NRHP Archive Search Results for Covered Bridges of Georgia on National Registry of Historic Places." npgallery.nps.gov/NRHP/SearchResults?view=list.

Orr, Eleanor. "Covered Bridge at New Location." *Columbus [GA] Ledger*, September 6, 1965, 11.

Osinski, Bill. "Magic Land of Mansions and Artist Colonies." *Atlanta Constitution*, March 15, 1998, 76.

Pantone, Milo. "Auchumpkee Creek Covered Bridge (Thomaston, Ga)." YouTube. July 26, 2022. youtu.be/IIhYKdXiI6c.

Patureau, Alan. "The Bridges of Georgia." *Atlanta Journal*, June 21, 1995, 35.

Petersen, Hegen. *Kissing Bridges*. VT: Stephen Greene Press, 1965.

Post, Audrey. "Spanning Time." *Macon [GA] Telegraph*, October 27, 1985, 49.

Sandy Earon, Aha-Media. "Concord Covered Bridge, Smyrna Georgia." Georgia's Most Popular Recreational Travel and Events Guide. www.n-georgia.com/concord-bridge.htm.

Sivell, Shiann. "Welcome Home: Bridge Built by Horace King and Sons Returns to Troup County after Nearly 60 Years." *LaGrange [GA] Daily News*, February 23, 2022. www.lagrangenews.com/2022/02/23/welcome-home-bridge-built-by-horace-king-and-sons-returns-home-after-nearly-60-years.

Sparks, Andrew. "Long Bridge on Broad River." *Atlanta Journal and Constitution*, n.d.

Tanner, Michael. "Coheelee Creek Covered Bridge." Clio. theclio.com/entry/6445.

Thomaston-Upson Chamber of Commerce, GA. "Auchumpkee Creek Covered Bridge." Last modified 2022. www.thomastongachamber.com/auchumpkee-creek-covered-bridge.

Travis, Dale J. "Georgia Covered Bridges List." Round Barns and Covered Bridges. Last modified September 2022. www.dalejtravis.com/cblist/cbga.htm.

———. "Georgia Numbers." Round Barns and Covered Bridges. Last modified March 17, 2023. www.dalejtravis.com/maps/numbers/ga.htm.

Two Egg. "Coheelee Creek Falls, Parts 1–4." YouTube. www.youtube.com/watch?v=KGKg1G2qblg;.

Urban Baboon. "Stovall Mill Covered Bridge." Last modified April 4, 2009. urbanbaboon.blogspot.com/2009/04/stovall-mill-covered-bridge.html.

U.S. Army Corps of Engineers, Mobile District. "West Point Lake." www.sam.usace.army.mil/Missions/Civil-Works/Recreation/West-Point-Lake.

U.S. National Park Service. "What Is the National Register of Historic Places?" Last modified October 25, 2022. www.nps.gov/subjects/nationalregister/what-is-the-national-register.htm.

Vardeman, Johnny. "Bridge Was More Than Just a Way to Cross River." *Gainesville [GA] Times*, December 8, 2007. www.gainesvilletimes.com/

columnists/johnny-vardemans-column/bridge-was-more-than-just-a-way-to-cross-river.

WRBL. "Historic Covered Bridge Returns to Troup County." Last modified February 23, 2022. www.wrbl.com/news/georgia-news/historic-covered-bridge-returns-to-troup-county.

WSB-TV. "Covered Bridge Put in Place in Stone Mountain Park." Workform: Brown Media Archive Newsfilm Database:wsbn47875, March 17, 1965. dbsmaint.galib.uga.edu/cgi/news?query=id%3Awsbn47875.

WTVM. "Historic Bridge Returns to LaGrange after 57 Years." Last modified February 22, 2022. www.wtvm.com/2022/02/22/historic-bridge-returns-lagrange-after-57-years.

YouTube. "The Auchumpkee Creek Covered Bridge." Keeping History on Two Wheels. November 29, 2020. www.youtube.com/watch?v=j936ec0QzME.

———. "Blind Susie Lula Covered Bridge." January 10, 2010. www.youtube.com/watch?v=nuhenzpzL24.

———. "Coheelee Covered Bridge." March 31, 2021. www.youtube.com/watch?v=KGKg1G2qblg.

———. "Coheelee Creek Bridge." www.youtube.com/watch?v=UN_hpCFooZ4.

———. "Coheelee Creek Falls Parks 1, 2, 3." March 31, 2021. www.youtube.com/watch?v=KGKg1G2qblg.

———. "Ghost Hunting on the Stovall Mill Covered Bridge Near Helen, Georgia." Last modified February 13, 2019. www.youtube.com/watch?v=Qcm3mXYVAP8.

———. "The Goat-Man of Coheelee Creek Covered Bridge." March 4, 2020. www.YouTube.com/watch?v=D7HhiQLs4B4.

———. "Restoring Georgia's Covered Bridges." November 7, 2016. www.youtube.com/watch?v=TFlfa7_CY7E.